Assessing Faculty Publication Productivity
Issues of Equity

by Elizabeth G. Creamer

ASHE-ERIC Higher Education Report Volume 26, Number 2

Prepared by

ERIC*THE*

ERIC Clearinghouse on Higher Education
The George Washington University
URL: www.gwu.edu/~eriche

In cooperation with

ASHE

Association for the Study
of Higher Education
URL: http://www.tiger.coe.missouri.edu/~ashe

Published by

The
George
Washington
University
WASHINGTON DC

Graduate School of Education and Human Development
The George Washington University
URL: www.gwu.edu

Jonathan D. Fife, Series Editor

Cite as

Creamer, Elizabeth G. 1998. *Assessing Faculty Publication Productivity: Issues of Equity.* ASHE-ERIC Higher Education Report Volume 26, No. 2. Washington, D.C.: The George Washington University, Graduate School of Education and Human Development.

Library of Congress Catalog Card Number 98-84365
ISSN 0884-0040
ISBN 1-878380-82-6

Managing Editor: Lynne J. Scott
Manuscript Editor: Sandra Selva
Cover Design by Michael David Brown, Inc., The Red Door Gallery, Rockport, ME

The ERIC Clearinghouse on Higher Education invites individuals to submit proposals for writing monographs for the *ASHE-ERIC Higher Education Report* series. Proposals must include:
1. A detailed manuscript proposal of not more than five pages.
2. A chapter-by-chapter outline.
3. A 75-word summary to be used by several review committees for the initial screening and rating of each proposal.
4. A vita and a writing sample.

ERIC Clearinghouse on Higher Education
Graduate School of Education and Human Development
The George Washington University
One Dupont Circle, Suite 630
Washington, DC 20036-1183

> *The mission of the ERIC system is to improve American education by increasing and facilitating the use of educational research and information on practice in the activities of learning, teaching, educational decision making, and research, wherever and whenever these activities take place.*

This publication was prepared partially with funding from the Office of Educational Research and Improvement, U.S. Department of Education, under contract no. ED RR-93-002008. The opinions expressed in this report do not necessarily reflect the positions or policies of OERI or the Department.

EXECUTIVE SUMMARY

Faculty publishing productivity is often used as an index of departmental and institutional prestige and is strongly associated with an individual faculty member's reputation, visibility, and advancement in the academic reward structure, particularly at research institutions. Lower levels of scholarly productivity, as reflected by quantity of publications, is one explanation that focuses on why women and minorities have not progressed more rapidly in the academic reward structure; why they continue to be promoted at slower and lower rates than majority, male academics; and why they are concentrated in less prestigious institutions. Understanding the factors associated with publishing productivity and how gender and race are insinuated in traditional criteria, used to assess faculty research productivity, can assist academic administrators in defining methods of shaping institutional reward structures in ways that advance the careers of a heterogenous faculty.

An overwhelming amount of research has been published about faculty research performance. A subset of this literature addresses variations by gender and race in publication productivity and the impact of the criteria used to measure it. This study provides a synthesis of the research literature about how gender is a factor in publishing productivity. The discussion extends John Creswell's 1985 ASHE-ERIC Higher Education Report on faculty research performance by summarizing the literature, produced since its publication, and in the focus on the role of gender.

The literature about gender differences in faculty productivity is grounded in the work of a group of scholars, primarily in sociology and the sociology of science, who have contributed to the study of women's success in science careers and to stratification in higher education. It is supplemented by the insights of feminists exploring the experiences of academic women and the feminist critique of traditional measures of research productivity.

This study explores publication productivity, not other aspects of faculty work performance, such as teaching or service. The focus is on faculty, because they produce the majority of scholarly publications at doctoral granting institutions.

In addition to those initiating research in the area, academics, such as department heads or deans, who have oversight for promotion and tenure decisions, will find the topic of faculty publishing productivity to be relevant. It is most germane to settings where research and scholarly publications are considered central to rewards. It will be particularly useful for academics who are called to judge the records of colleagues in a number of academic fields, as well as those trying to understand the broader context of their own publishing productivity.

There are several major questions about gender and race differences in faculty publishing productivity:

Are there significant gender and race differences in publishing productivity?

Although there are large variations by discipline, the majority of male and female faculty members at four-year institutions produce a dozen or fewer articles in academic or professional journals over their careers. While gender differences in average publication rates appear to have narrowed in many fields (Blackburn and Lawrence 1996), particularly when a relatively short time frame is used for study, women are significantly less likely than men to be among the top producers of publications in their fields. This small group of highly prolific writers account for a large proportion of the literature produced in an academic field (Cole and Singer 1991). The relative absence of the voices of women and minorities in widely cited literature is explained in part by the fact that few women and minorities are among prolific authors. Their under-representation among the prolific, and over-representation among nonpublishers, is the major reason for the characterization of faculty women being less productive than faculty men.

How are traditional measures of publication quantity and quality influenced by gender?

On average, gender differences in institutional rewards, such as tenure and salary, remain even when publishing productivity is controlled. In other words, women generally receive fewer resources and recognition than men for comparable productivity (Long and Fox 1995). This leads to the conclusion that stratification in science, or the concentration of women and minorities in the lower ranks, and at less prestigious institutions, cannot fully be justified by the assumption that impersonal, universal criteria are equitably applied (Long and Fox 1995).

What explains why such a small group of faculty are prolific?

Although the number of women is minuscule, prolific male and female publishers probably are more similar than dissimilar. Prolific writers are generally senior scholars at doctoral granting institutions whose interest in research, work assignment, and access to resources have coalesced to support a commitment to research that is sustained over decades. Many widely recognized authors who have made a substantial contribution to the knowledge in an academic field, such as through a noteworthy book, are not prolific writers.

Institutional policies and practices contribute, but do not determine, whether a faculty member initiates and sustains a substantial record of scholarly publishing. The value awarded to scholarly publishing in the institutional reward structure is most instrumental in determining whether a faculty member initiates a publishing record early in his or her career as a faculty member. The institution plays the most significant role in helping a faculty member to sustain a commitment to publishing through a work assignment. Time devoted to research and interest in research are stronger predictors of career research productivity than the institutional reward structure, including salary (Dill 1986).

Factors that are external to the institution play a central role to sustaining the productivity of prolific scholars, and colleagues who are external to the institution are the primary source of recognition and reinforcement for prolific writers. Lack of engagement in influential networks is one reason that the institutional reward structure may be even more influential to women's productivity than it is to men's.

Why are so few women and minorities among those who are prolific?

Prolific writers are disproportionately likely to be white males because the primary criteria used to define productivity, quantity of journal articles and citations to them, reflect career paths, work assignments, interests, and access to resources that are much more characteristic of white men than most women and minorities. This suggests that, in addition to examining the question of whether traditional productivity criteria are equitably applied, it is essential to examine the question of whether productivity criteria are equitable.

What are the implications for practice?

A major implication from a synthesis of the research literature is the suggestion that one way to create a more heterogenous faculty is to recognize a broad range of scholarly
activities, such as making a contribution to the production
and communication of knowledge. Diversifying the faculty
in the United States requires diversifying the criteria used to
judge their work performance. Traditional measures of impact or utility of publications, such as citations, must be expanded to recognize that academics are just one of many
communities that are impacted by the production of new
knowledge. New, convenient methods are needed to assess
the impact of a variety of forms of scholarly communication,
such as through unpublished works, conferences, presentations, speeches, and the ever expanding electronic venues
of communication.

There is almost no research about variations by race, and
the correlates of publishing productivity, to substantiate the
hypothesis that traditional measures of publishing productivity
impact all or some minorities in the same ways they have
been suggested in this text to impact faculty women. The characteristics, of those acknowledged as authorities, can be explored by assessing the extent that collegial networks and the
communication of knowledge is gender and race segregated.

CONTENTS

FOREWORD

There are only 24 hours in the day. Why is it then that some faculty are very successful in achieving a remarkable level of productivity and some produce little or nothing? Why is it that some institutions always seem to have high producing faculty and some are always what-to-bees? The answer is simple, productivity is no accident. It is the result—sometimes positive, sometimes negative—of how an institution values publishing productivity and what adjustments the institution is willing to make, on a faculty-by-faculty basis, to ensure that productivity.

One startling finding in John W. Creswell's 1985 ASHE-ERIC Higher Education Report on faculty research performance was that five years after a high producing faculty member was hired by a low producing program, either that faculty member had moved on to another institution or had lowered their productivity to be at the same level as her or his colleagues. While it may be true that proven past non-performers will be future non-performers, the reverse is not true. Like water seeking its own level, the productivity of faculty is greatly influenced by the productivity support processes or systems of their academic program.

Like all processes or systems, there are a multitude of factors that interrelate to produce the end results. First, there are the inputs resources. Faculty hired from high producing institutions with records of productivity are more likely to be future high producers.

Emphasis on providing student financial aid through research assistantships (to assist faculty in their scholarship), rather than graduate assistantships (to help in administrative duties) or teaching assistantships (to supplement classroom demands), will create a supportive resource for productivity. Guaranteed funding for both faculty and student travel to conduct research and to deliver papers at the national and regional conferences provides a sense of being valued that contributes to greater productivity efforts.

Second are the conditions that make up the productivity process. High producing institutions and programs almost always are respectful of the 24-hour clock by ensuring reasonable expectations and balance for teaching, institutional and student service activities, and scholarly productivity. Faculty are treated as individuals. At any one time, some faculty are more ready or positioned to be productive than other faculty. The secret is to recognize these high productivity periods and be supportive. The secret is also to recognize when a faculty member is ready for their next productivity phase and to provide supports, such as release teaching time, mentoring, or development opportunities that will give them the boost to achieve this growth.

It is the combination of input resources and process and system support that helps to produce the productivity culture of an academic program. However, while the formula seems to be simple the execution for many faculty, especially for women, has been very inconsistent. This inconsistency is a direct result of the primary academic leaders, deans, and department chairs, not knowing how this formula fits together and how to make it work for their faculty.

To help in understanding this formula is the mission of this Report. Elizabeth G. Creamer, associate professor of Women's Studies in the Center for Interdisciplinary at Virginia Polytechnic Institute and State University and adjunct in the higher education and student affairs program, has conducted an insightful analysis of the factors that influence publication productivity in general and what is specifically important for women faculty. Dr. Creamer begins her examination by reviewing the general nature of faculty publishing and then looks at how rewards and assessment of publishing performance influence productivity. Next, the author creates a conceptual understanding for the gender differences in publishing productivity. While throughout the Report the author carefully highlights the implications for practice for each section, the concluding section focuses on specific strategies that academic leaders can use to help create high publication productivity in all their faculty.

High productivity can be treated as a wish or an accident waiting to happen. It can be the result of the very few who are highly motivated or choose to seek recognition and appreciation outside their institution. Or, it can be part of a purposeful plan to create an organizational culture that is thoughtful, supportive, and expecting of high publishing productivity. For those who choose the latter, this Report will be of considerable help.

Jonathan D. Fife
Series Editor,
Professor of Higher Education Administration, and
Director, ERIC Clearinghouse on Higher Education

INTRODUCTION

Having always revered writers, while spending considerable time reading autobiographies by women, an interest in the topic of gender differences in faculty publishing productivity was discovered when reviewing a list of names of the most frequently cited authors in the field of higher education (Budd 1990). Despite the long history of women in education, it did not contain the name of a single woman. This launched an exploration of qualitative research about why so few women are among the most prolific scholarly women writers (Creamer 1994, 1995, 1996; Creamer and Engstrom 1996). The voices of more than 80 faculty, interviewed about their publication productivity in the last five years, have provided the core of understanding, relating to the intricacies of scholarly writing.

Audience
This text synthesizes and interprets the research literature about faculty publication productivity for academics who evaluate the publishing credentials of colleagues. The primary audience for the manuscript is academics involved in making decisions about faculty hiring and promotion. An additional audience is those beginning to do research on the topic of gender differences in publishing productivity. Those aspiring to be faculty and faculty women interested in understanding the broader context of publishing productivity measures will find the text particularly relevant, if not always encouraging.

Purpose
The major purpose of the text is to offer a synthesis of the research literature about gender differences in publishing productivity and in the correlates of publishing productivity. A deliberate attempt has been made to include citations about faculty productivity from a wide range of academic fields, in order to include an audience from disciplines that are both applied and basic. To the extent possible, with the limited amount of published material available, this discussion is extended to consider the same issues regarding race or ethnicity.

This text adds to research literature by enlarging the discussion of the conceptual explanations for gender differences among prolific publishers. The discussion extends John Creswell's publication, *Faculty Research Performance,* by the synthesis of the literature published since 1985 and its more detailed exploration of the factors associated with gender differences in long-term publishing productivity. It presents a critique of traditional measures of faculty productivity without venturing in any detail into the research literature about the far more encompassing issue of women's achievement and careers in science that also has a home in the sociology of science. It adds some feminists voices, such as Kirsch (1993), who are not generally cited in the research literature on the topic. This work has been most influenced by Kathryn B. Ward, Linda Grant, and J. Scott Long; they are all sociologists who have done a substantial amount of publishing over an extended period of time on the topic of gender and academic publishing.

Language Usage

In the research literature, it is common practice to utilize the expression, "research productivity," when referring to publishing productivity. In this text, the expression of faculty publishing productivity has been used, because it clearly identifies the aspect of faculty performance that is under scrutiny. Traditional language obscures the underlying assumption that teaching, service, and research are mutually compatible aspects of faculty performance and that all three roles are elements of a single dimension. This is the logic that justifies evaluating faculty performance primarily through scholarly publications. Part of the purpose of this review is to deconstruct traditional measures of faculty productivity and to analyze their implications for women and minorities.

Similarly, the distinction between the terms, reinforcement, reward, and recognition are made, although many authors in the literature use them interchangeably when referring to the interactive feedback processes that sustain long-term scholarly productivity.

How the Book Is Organized

The first three chapters rely heavily on the research literature since 1985, with older citations provided only when they are particularly relevant to findings reported in the research literature about gender and race differences in the factors associated with publishing productivity. The first chapter is used to describe patterns of faculty scholarly publishing productivity and how these vary by sex, race, and academic field. The second chapter reviews the evidence from the research literature of the relationship between publication productivity and institutional rewards, and how these vary by gender and race. Traditional measures of the quantity and quality of publication productivity and a discussion about whether these measures are universally applied without consideration of gender, appears in the third chapter. Because the chapters are meant to stand alone to some extent, each closes with a summary and a discussion of the implications for practice.

A summary of conceptual explanations for gender differences in publishing productivity is provided in Chapter 4, organized under the categories of individual characteristics, institutional factors, environmental factors, and the cumulative advantage perspective.

Moving from the literature in the final two chapters to apply the conceptual model, an explanation has been developed to examine the gender gap in the long term and to determine the implications for practice and research in career publication productivity. In Chapter 5, proposed characteristics include prolific scholarly publishers, using the categories presented in the previous chapter. A summary of implications for practice and for future research appear in Chapter 6. Support for conclusions and interpretations offered in these two, final chapters are developed in the preceding chapters. Readers most interested in the conceptual aspects of the topic may choose just to read the last several chapters, but they will find most of the supporting citations in earlier chapters.

Readers primarily interested in the implications for practice, will find it most expedient to only read the summary and implications for practice sections that appear at the end of each chapter and all of Chapter 6. The last chapter is written so that it might be reproduced, with appropriate citation, and distributed to members of promotion and tenure committees.

Major Conclusions

Several major conclusions weave in and out of the text. The first is that, particularly when analyzed over the course of a career, publishing productivity should not be viewed as exclusively the product of individual qualities, such as ability and interest in research. In terms of the way a researcher would express it, race and gender do not have a direct effect on publishing productivity, but an indirect effect through factors, such as rank and academic field; institutional factors, including a work assignment; and by environmental factors, such as access to funding and influential collegial networks. The factors that initiate publishing productivity are not identical to those that sustain a commitment to publishing, although some of the initial factors, such as collaboration with an influential mentor, have a long-term impact on productivity. Gender and race differences in the development of publishing productivity are small, but have a long-term, cumulative impact (Long 1990).

The second major issue raised in the text relates to two aspects of the issue of universalism. It is one of the four norms of sciences proposed by Merton (Braxton 1993), which is the assumption that criteria for judging scientific merit are impersonal and universal—meaning that they are applied without regard to functionally irrelevant characteristics, such as race or gender. One of the major points raised in this text: There is ample evidence of these measures not being applied without regard to gender. A second issue is the even more substantive challenge that traditional criteria of measuring faculty publishing productivity are weighted inequitably, because they disproportionately impact women and minorities in a negative way. Park (1996) made this point when she observed that traditional criteria for faculty productivity should primarily function, not to distinguish between the men and the boys, but between the men and the women.

A major argument raised in the text is that the profile of faculty across the country has remained so stubbornly homogeneous because of the reluctance to relinquish traditional measures of faculty productivity, in that they are considered to be applied with universalistic (scientific merit), rather than particularistic (selective) criteria. A narrow definition of what constitutes a contribution to knowledge represents only a fragment of academic discourse, and it awards the privilege of an authoritative voice to only a few scholars. Expanding these definitions will benefit minority, female, and male academics alike.

THE NATURE OF FACULTY PUBLISHING PRODUCTIVITY

College and university-level academic administrators and those heading cross-disciplinary or interdisciplinary units may not fully be aware of how scholarly publishing practices vary by academic field. The purpose of this chapter is to describe faculty scholarly publishing productivity across academic fields and how these vary by gender and race. The factors that contribute to publishing productivity and how these vary by gender are discussed in Chapter 4.

Defining Publishing Productivity

It is not difficult to find articles in the journals of almost any academic field or discipline to determine how scholars define scholarly productivity. A summary of criteria used to assess publishing productivity in 11 journal articles in nine different academic fields is shown in Table 1.1. The table includes only a small proportion of the articles about scholarly productivity published since 1985. Articles were selected to illustrate how publishing productivity was assessed in a range of academic fields. Some articles, such as Bayer and Smart's (1991) are excluded because the sample included only male academics, while other research is excluded because average productivity levels are not disaggregated by gender. The literature about scholarly productivity before 1985 is summarized by other sources (Creswell 1985; Finkelstein 1984).

The criteria used to measure publishing productivity in the research literature is relatively consistent across many academic fields. Quantity of journal articles or publications are the two measures used to assess publishing productivity. Table 1.1 illustrates that while both measures are used in the research literature, the number of journal articles is used most frequently to assess faculty research productivity. Quantity of journal articles is used more widely than any other measure in the research literature about scholarly productivity (Astin 1991; Ward and Grant 1996). They are relatively easy to measure, and are presumed to reflect the production of new knowledge or research productivity; they are valued in almost all disciplines, except the visual and performing arts where other measures of scholarship apply.

Data to calculate publication output is generally collected from one of two sources. The first method is through self-reported data which has been found to be highly reliable (Creswell 1985). The second method utilizes indices published in many fields that abstract articles published by year

TABLE 1.1

**Criteria Used to Assess Publishing Productivity
From Representative Studies, By Field**

Field/ Source	Productivity Measure		Source of Data About Publications
	# Journal Articles	# of Publications	
Accountants			
Omundson and Mann (1994)	X		Accountant's Index, 1973-1989
Biochemists			
Long (1990)	X		Chemical Abstracts
Communications			
Hickson et al. (1993)	X		Index to Journals in Communication Studies, 1986-1990
Economists			
Hutchinson and Zivny (1995)	X		126 journals
Journalism and Mass Communications			
Dupagne (1993)		X	journal articles, books
Library Sciences			
Garland (1990)		X	Weighted score of monographs, textbooks, articles, book chapters
Korytnyk (1985)		X	Monographs, chapters, articles, papers, pamphlets compiled in Library Literature
Physical Education			
Knoppers (1989)	X		11 research based journals
Social Scientists			
Davis and Astin (1987)		X	self reported, articles, books, chapters
Social Work			
Fox and Faver (1985)	X		self reported, articles published or accepted for publication
Schiele (1991)	X		self reported, career total

and author from selected refereed journals. These are now available in electronic form.

A number of agencies conduct national surveys of faculty that include cumulative or career measures of publishing productivity. These include: the Carnegie Foundation for the Advancement of Teaching, the American Council of Education (ACE), the National Center for Research to Improve Postsecondary Teaching and Learning (NCRIPTAL), and the Higher Education Research Institute (HERI). These surveys provide a portrait of faculty attitude and behaviors, including levels of publishing productivity, and how these have changed over time.

Average Faculty Publication Rates

Table 1.2 displays gender differences in the mean journal article productivity by academic field reported in some of the empirical studies listed in Table 1.1. Some articles listed in the first

TABLE 1.2

Gender Differences in Mean Journal Article Productivity, By Field; Reported in Representative Studies, By Field

Field/ Source	Time Frame	Mean Article Productivity		
		Men	Women	P
Accountants Omundson and Mann (1994)	8 years prior to promotion	3.11	2.35	N.S.
Biochemists Long (1990)	3 years predoctoral	1.93	1.53	**
Journalism Dupagne (1993)	yearly career average	1.12	.53	***
Library Sciences Garland (1990) Korytnyk (1985)	5 years 5 years following Ph.D.	1.66 4.20	1.27 1.80	N.S. **
Physical Education Knoppers (1989)	5 years	1.88	1.69	N.S.
Social Work Fox and Faver (1985)	2 yrs prior to survey	2.1	1.63	*

Notes: * = $p < .10$; ** = $p < .05$; *** = $p < .001$
N.S. = not significant

table are not shown in the second table, because data on gender differences on the indices of productivity are not presented in the article. Because some data are not duplicated across the tables, Table 1.2 is best read in conjunction with Table 1.1.

Consistent with what is suggested by Table 1.2, no significant gender differences are reported in the two-year publication rate in 1988 of faculty in eight disciplines (Bentley and Blackburn 1992). Women averaged 2.8 publications and men 3.1 publications in a two-year period. The gender gap in publication productivity had narrowed between 1969 and 1988 in biology, psychology, and English (see tables in Blackburn and Lawrence 1996, p. 50-51). Although the rationale for the selection of the eight disciplines is not explained in either source, faculty in a broad range of disciplines were studied, including: humanities (English, history), natural sciences (biology, chemistry, mathematics) and social sciences (political science, psychology, sociology). When a small unit of time is utilized, differences between male and female productivity are generally found to be quite small, although almost always in favor of men.

Although this is not discernable from the information displayed in Table 1.2, average faculty publication rates vary sharply by institutional type. Publication rates of faculty at research institutions are about double of the overall rates (Blackburn and Lawrence 1996).

Nonpublishers
One of the phenomena that has intrigued researchers so much that it has been labeled the "productivity puzzle" (Cole and Singer 1991; Cole and Zuckerman 1984; Creswell 1985) is the large percentage of faculty who either never publish or who have only produced a few publications, despite the strong emphasis on sharing the results of research in the norms of science. Slightly more than one-fourth of the faculty reported that they had never produced a journal article that was published in an academic or professional journal (Boyer 1990). This number is misleading, though, because there are wide variations by field, and it includes faculty at institutions where they are not expected to publish, as well as faculty who were hired before scholarly publications were part of the institutional reward structure. About three times more women than men faculty at research universities reported

they had never published an article in an academic or professional journal (Astin, Day, and Korn 1991).

One of the explanations for gender differences in aggregate levels of productivity is that women are significantly
more likely than men to be among the nonpublishers (Long
1992). Findings about differences in the proportion of nonpublishers among faculty in all disciplines are quite consistent in two recent surveys of faculty. About 23 percent of the
men and 43 percent of the women from the 1989 HERI Faculty Survey (Astin et al. 1991), and 22 percent of the men
and 36 percent of the women from the 1989 National Survey
of Faculty (Boyer 1990) by the Carnegie Foundation
reported that they had never published an article in a professional or academic journal.

Evidence that Faculty Publication Rates Are Increasing
Average faculty publication rates have increased substantially
in the last 25 years at all types of institutions, as has the
number of faculty expressing an interest in research (Bentley
and Blackburn 1990; Blackburn and Lawrence 1996). Evidence of this comes from comparing findings from the national faculty surveys over time. For example, findings from
the 1972-1973 ACE survey of faculty indicated that 12 percent of the women and 35 percent of the men had published a cumulative total of five or more articles in scholarly
journals (Bayer and Astin 1975). In comparison, 65 percent
of the women and 78 percent of the men had published five
or more articles over the course of their careers, according
to a 1989 survey by the Carnegie Foundation (Boyer 1990).

A variety of factors are associated with the increase in
level of faculty publishing productivity rates. More institutions are giving weight to scholarly publications in their hiring and promotion practices, because the number of candidates for faculty positions far exceed the number of available positions (Schuster and Bowen 1985). The number of
pages available in journals have increased in some fields,
such as biology and psychology, while decreasing in others,
such as English (Bieber and Blackburn 1993). It was calculated that between 1972 and 1988, available pages in journals for each faculty member almost doubled in psychology,
more than doubled in biology, and declined by almost 50
percent in English (Bieber and Blackburn 1993). Shortage

of journal space depresses faculty publishing levels in some academic fields.

Publication Rates By Field

Average levels of publication productivity vary widely between academic fields, as well as within subspecialties in the same disciplinary grouping. Disciplines with the highest average, career publication rates are cellular and molecular biology, physics, biochemistry, psychology, and chemistry (Baird 1991). These might be characterized as high-consensus fields or fields with high paradigmatic development. These are fields where there is relatively widespread agreement about the central research paradigm; meaning that there is consensus about what are the important research questions and the major theories and methods (Braxton and Hargens 1996). These are often referred to as the "hard" sciences (Biglan 1973). However, there are substantial variations in publishing rates, even within disciplinary groups, as well as across programs (Baird 1991). For example, mean two-year productivity rates among programs in psychology were almost double of those for history and political science which are also in the social sciences (Baird 1991).

Academic fields with the highest percentages of faculty across institutional types, who published 11 or more journal articles over the course of their careers, include engineering, biological sciences, and physical sciences (see Table A-19 in Boyer 1990). Health science faculty have the highest average number of career refereed journals articles—26.6 (Mooney 1991, p. A17). Book publication rates are highest among faculty in the humanities and social sciences (see Table A-20 in Boyer 1990). Social scientists produce more books and journal articles than humanists (Wanner, Lewis, and Gregorio 1981). Some of the gender and race differences noted in scholarly productivity are related to the fact that women and minorities are concentrated in academic areas where journal article publication is not generally very high.

There are substantial differences in the nature and average length of journal articles among academic fields which further restrict the ability to make generalizations across disciplines about average levels of faculty productivity. For example, 10 to 12 journal articles a year is not uncommon in chemistry where publications are often less than 4,000 words, while faculty in math average about one-half that number and publications are only about half that long (Becher 1989). The publications of faculty in the natural and physical sciences generally focus on a few key, highly specialized topics over the course of an academic career, and they tend to be conducted by teams of researchers, while relying heavily on institutional resources and external funding (Becher 1989). Invited working papers are among the most prestigious forms of publications in many fields (Ward and Grant 1996).

Faculty publication rates are affected by the acceptance rates of journals in their academic field. Journals in different disciplinary fields vary substantially in the proportion of manuscripts they accept for publication, the average number of revisions required, and the length of time to publication (Hargens 1990). In a study of 30 journals, the average annual acceptance rates ranged from a low of 11 percent in two journals in political science and sociology to a high of more than 80 percent in several journals in chemistry (Hargens 1988). Also, there is a determination of an acceptance rate of 91 percent in a journal in the physical sciences, 59 percent in the biological sciences, and 13 percent in the social sciences. The conclusion is that the disciplinary differences in the number of referees, associated with the amount of consensus in the field, influenced acceptance rates far more than shortage of space in the journals (Hargens 1990). Acceptance rates are higher among journals in the high-consensus academic areas where there is a central research paradigm and where articles tend to be relatively short, such as chemistry (Ward and Grant 1996).

There are a number of additional characteristics of an academic field that influence average rates of publishing productivity. These include: the number of journals, equipment and resources required to conduct research, rate of obsolescence of knowledge, patterns of collaboration, opportunities to publish nonmainstream research, and the role of invited pieces (Ward and Grant 1996). Average journal publication rates are highest among faculty in the high-consensus academic fields where there are many journals, acceptance rates for articles are relatively high, and articles are relatively short with multiple co-authors. An increase in the number of articles in scientific journals with the astonishing number of more than 100 co-authors has been documented (McDonald 1995).

The methods of research, topics of research, and patterns of authorship selected by men are more likely than those selected by women to be compatible with publication guidelines of the most prestigious journals (Ward and Grant 1996). Women's published work is more likely than men's published work to focus on topics considered to be nonmainstream and personal, to be cross- disciplinary, and to avoid theory (Aisenberg and Harrington 1988). Women are significantly less likely than men to serve as sole or lead authors which are positions that in most, but not all, academic fields offer higher status, prestige, and reward by virtue of being assumed to reflect senior status. Women generally receive less recognition or credit than do men for their contribution to a co-authored piece, particularly with a senior male (Sonnert and Holton, 1995b; Ward and Grant 1996).

Productivity Rates of Prolific Faculty
Top-producing faculty who have sustained relatively high levels of publishing productivity over the course of a career are often labeled in the research literature as prolific scholars. While the number of nonproducers increases over the career span, the highest producers tend to start writing and publish-

TABLE 1.3

Percentage of Faculty Women and Men, By Level of Journal Article Productivity and By Institutional Type*

Number of Journal	All Institutions		Universities	
Articles	Women	Men	Women	Men
None	43.3	22.9	19.6	6.7
1 - 2	22.7	17.2	8.8	8.8
3 - 4	12.9	13.1	16.2	10.8
5 - 10	11.3	16.2	19.1	18.4
11 - 20	6.1	12.5	15.7	19.4
21 - 50	3.0	11.9	7.7	21.9
51 +	.7	6.2	2.0	14.1

*Source: 1989 HERI Faculty Survey (Astin, Korn, and Day 1991).

ing early in their careers and to remain relatively stable publishers over time (Blackburn, Behymer, and Hall 1978). In all institutions, less than 1 percent of the women faculty and about 6 percent of the men faculty reported they had published a career total of 51 or more articles in academic or professional journals (see Table 1.3 in Astin et al. 1991).

Prolific faculty are usually described in the research literature as being among the top 3 percent to 5 percent of their profession in terms of the number of published journal articles. In some academic fields, generally those with a low level of paradigmatic development, the total number of publications required to achieve this appellation may seem quite small. Social sciences is a disciplinary grouping where rejection rates for articles are relatively high when compared to high consensus fields, such as in the physical sciences (Hargens 1998). For example, of the published research about career productivity in different academic fields in the social sciences, one author identified the top 3.6 percent of the active publishers in communication studies, as those with a total of 11 or more articles indexed in the Index to Journals in Communication Studies (Hickson, Stacks, and Amsbary 1993). Those who had produced 21 or more articles over the course of a career are identified as the top 5 percent of faculty in the social sciences (Davis and Astin 1987). The top 2 percent of the contributors to seven journals in higher education were distinguished as those who had published four or more articles in a five year period (Hunter 1986; Hunter and Kuh 1987).

Prolific faculty account for the majority of publications in an academic field. Although percentages vary by field, it is generally estimated that about 15 percent of the faculty produce about 50 percent of the publications (Long and Fox 1995). For example, in the biological, physical, and social sciences, 15 percent of the faculty accounted for 50 percent of the publications in those fields (J.R. Cole 1979). It is estimated that less than 30 percent of the higher education faculty account for 75 percent of the research published in the field (Hunter and Kuh 1987). Because they are so few in number, prolific women account for a higher percentage of publications by women than prolific men account for publications by men (Cole and Zuckerman 1984). Among a matched sample of scientists in the biological and physical scientists, it is observed that 15 percent of the men accounted for 49 percent of the journal articles published by men, while

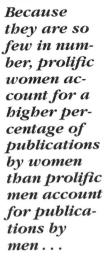

Because they are so few in number, prolific women account for a higher percentage of publications by women than prolific men account for publications by men . . .

15 percent of the women accounted for 57 percent of the articles published by women (Cole and Zuckerman 1984).

Gender and Publishing Productivity

There has been considerable debate in the literature about the role of gender in publishing productivity. An "overwhelming evidence" is found from dozens of studies in the 1970s that men out-publish women (Finkelstein 1984). Similarly, findings from more than 50 studies of scientists in a variety of fields showed the same conclusion (Cole and Zuckerman 1984). Based on an analysis of the 12-year productivity rate of a matched sample of male and female scientists in astronomy, biochemistry, chemistry, earth sciences, mathematics, and physics, it is calculated that female scientists produced about two-thirds of the articles of male scientists (Cole and Zuckerman 1984). It is observed that, although there were variations across studies, "within a given period, women publish about half as many articles as men" (Fox 1985, p. 263).

As shown in Table 1.2, some studies published since 1985 document significant gender differences in average productivity rates in certain fields, while some do not. For instance, significant gender differences in publishing productivity were reported among journalism and mass communication educators (Dupagne 1993), social work faculty (Fox and Faver 1985), library faculty (Korytnyk 1988), and among biochemists (Long 1990). On the other hand, no significant gender differences in the publication rate of physical educators were found (Knoppers (1989). Male and female faculty in library and information sciences were deemed equally as productive (Garland 1990), and no gender differences were found in the publication rates of male and female accountants (Omundson and Mann 1994).

Some of the differences in the findings about gender and publishing productivity are related to the unit of time utilized for the analysis. It is noted that significant gender differences in publishing productivity generally do not appear when short periods of time, such as two years, are utilized for the comparison, but tend to emerge only when longer units of time are considered (Cole and Singer 1991). Consistent with that conclusion, longitudinal studies of cohorts of male and female scientists, matched by year of doctorate and discipline, consistently report significant gender differences in productivity (Zuckerman and Cole 1984; Long 1992).

*Observations of small fragments in time of the careers
of men and women scientists, whose initial conditions
at the start of graduate school are roughly the same, re-
veal virtually no distinctions in productivity by sex. It is
the cumulative, long-term nature of the development of
productivity and, in turn, reward differentials that
represent the challenge for an explanatory theory* (Cole
and Singer 1991, p. 279).

Without question, gender differences in levels of publishing productivity are reduced when factors strongly related to
productivity, such as institutional location, are controlled
(Blackburn et al. 1978). Institutional location has the strongest
impact on publishing productivity in fields where research
requires substantial material resources (Wanner, Lewis, and
Gregorio 1981). The publication gap between men and
women faculty narrows substantially among those at the
same type of institution, with similar doctoral training, in the
same discipline, and at the same point in their careers (Ward
and Grant 1996). Except among the most prolific, recent studies have found that publishing rates, particularly over relatively short periods of time, among men and women faculty
in many academic fields, are converging (Ward and Grant
1996). However, this is not the case in all academic fields.

Some of what is found to be generally characteristic of
women faculty is described by at least one group of authors
(Blackburn et al. 1978) in the research literature as being
"exactly the opposite" (p. 138) of the characteristics most
often positively correlated with high productivity. More suc-
cinctly, when compared to men, women express less interest in research, are more likely to teach undergraduate than
graduate courses, less likely to graduate from prestigious
doctoral programs, more often untenured and at a lower
rank, and more likely to be in the humanities than the natural sciences (Blackburn et al. 1978). When the effects of
these variables are statistically controlled in research, gender
differences in career productivity often are substantially di-
minished or disappear. This illustrates the critical point that
the correlates of scholarly productivity are gender-related,
but gender is not a predictor or cause of publishing performance (Cole and Singer 1991). In other words, gender affects publication productivity indirectly through these correlates rather than being, directly or causally, related to pro-

ductivity. There are significant differences by gender in the correlates of scholarly productivity (Blackburn et al.1978). These are discussed in detail in the fourth chapter.

Gender and Prolific Publishing

Even at research universities, there is a large gap between the proportion of women and men faculty who have published a large number of articles in academic or professional journals. Table 1.3 displays data from the 1989 HERI Faculty Survey (Astin et al.1991) that compares the percentage of men and women faculty at all institutions and at universities by their self reported number of journal articles produced to date.

As illustrated in Table 1.3, which includes universities, the majority of both men and women faculty have produced a career total of fewer than 10 journal articles. A higher percentage of women than men faculty at universities have produced between three and 10 articles. The most dramatic gender difference in journal article productivity is clearly evident at either end of the range. When compared to men, a much larger proportion of women, even at research universities, are among nonpublishers and a much smaller proportion of women are among those who have published a great deal.

Race and Publishing Productivity

Unlike the topic of variations by gender in publishing productivity, very little has been published in research literature about race or ethnicity and level of publishing productivity or the correlates of publishing productivity, particularly during the time frame covered by this publication. In part, this may be explained by the fact that the proportion of minority faculty has and continues to be about 10 percent of the total population of faculty (Blackburn and Lawrence 1996). Many research studies are plagued by the difficulty of reaching any conclusions because sample sizes of minority participants are so small. As the correlates of men's and women's productivity differ, there is reason to believe that correlates of minority and majority faculty also are distinguishable (Blackburn, Wenzel, and Bieber 1994).

While there are distinct variations among members of different racial or ethnic groups, majority women and minority faculty share some attributes related to institutional and disciplinary location and academic rank associated with publishing productivity. For instance, a disproportionate number of African American faculty are employed in private liberal arts, public comprehensive, and two-year institutions, while Asian American faculty are at public and private research institutions in numbers that exceed their overall representation on the faculty across institutions (*The Chronicle of Higher Education Almanac Issue*, 1996).

As with women, most minority faculty are disproportionately located in disciplines that do not have particularly high levels of publishing productivity, as measured by journal articles. For instance, African American are disproportionately located in education and the social sciences and Hispanics in humanities. The exception are Asian American faculty who are located in engineering and the health and natural sciences (*The Chronicle of Higher Education Almanac Issue*, 1996).

Prolific publishers are generally senior faculty who have accumulated a large number of publications over the course of a 20- or 30-year career. As with white women faculty who are most likely to be found in the lower, instructional ranks, only 10 percent of full professors are members of a minority group and only 1.9 percent are minority women (*The Chronicle of Higher Education Almanac Issue*, 1996). Minority faculty are less likely to be tenured than either white male or female faculty (Blackburn et al. 1994). Faculty in senior ranks, particularly at research institutions, are more likely to have a work assignment that allows time for research than do faculty in more junior ranks.

Minority faculty share some additional characteristics with women faculty that are associated with low levels of publishing productivity. That includes the tendency to write on issues related to race or ethnicity which are generally difficult to publish in mainstream journals (Schiele 1991); less access to collaborative and mentoring relationships, particularly with majority faculty; location in ethnic studies programs; sources of stress related to personal and community life (Smith 1991); excessive institutional demands for service, and the perception that the works of African American writers are subjective and unscholarly (Schiele 1991). African American faculty reported conflict in playing by the rules of the game that focused on adding to the body of knowledge at the expense of making a contribution to the community (Robinson 1996).

Only a small number of journal articles have been published about differences by race or ethnicity in publishing productivity. Most articles report extremely modest or statisti-

As with women, most minority faculty are disproportionately located in disciplines that do not have particularly high levels of publishing productivity . . .

cally insignificant differences by race in level of publishing productivity within the same discipline and using a defined unit of time, rather than examining career productivity. For instance, Elmore and Blackburn (1983) found no significant differences in three-year publication rates of black and white faculty at Big 10 universities. Nettles and Perna (1995) reported no significant differences in the career publishing productivity of white, African American, and Asian American/ Pacific Islander faculty. Wanner et al. (1981) found that the significance of the relationship between race and career productivity disappeared when other factors were introduced in a regression equation for faculty in the social sciences and humanities, but remained statistically significant in the natural sciences. Similarly, Blackburn et al. (1994) found no statistically significant differences by race in two-year publication rates in 12 of 15 occupational fields.

Schiele (1991, 1992) and Pearson (1985) reported slightly different findings. African American social work faculty published slightly less than all social work doctorates but that a much higher percentage of them were among nonpublishers, and a much lower percentage were among the highest category of productivity (Schiele 1991, 1992). When comparing career publication productivity among academics in the physical, biological, and social scientists, the mean productivity of black faculty was found to be less than that of white faculty in all three fields (Pearson 1985). Part of the explanation is that, regardless of academic field, black respondents reported spending more time on teaching than white respondents (Pearson 1985). Publishing productivity is distributed unevenly among faculty, regardless of racial/ethnicity differences (Schiele 1992).

As with gender differences in publishing productivity, much of what appears to be substantial racial differences in levels of publishing productivity disappear when the comparison is limited to faculty in the same discipline, at similar institutions, at similar points of the career, and using time units of two to three years, rather than comparing total career productivity.

Summary

This chapter focused on a description of the nature of publication productivity in a variety of academic fields, including highlights of some of the gender and race differences in publishing productivity. Key points from this chapter are:

1. There are substantial differences in publication productivity across fields within a disciplinary area.
2. Faculty publishing productivity is almost always measured in terms of the number of journal articles produced in a given time frame.
3. Across all academic fields and institutions, faculty average about one publication a year.
4. About one-fourth of all faculty have never published a journal article in a refereed publication.
5. About 3 percent to 5 percent of all faculty are considered to be prolific.
6. Women faculty are significantly more likely than men faculty to be among nonpublishers and significantly less likely than men to be among the prolific.
7. Significant gender and race differences in publishing productivity are most likely to emerge when the unit of analysis is career productivity.
8. Gender and race do not predict scholarly productivity.
9. Significant gender and race differences exist in the correlates of scholarly productivity.

Implications for Practice
The summary of major trends in academic publishing have several major implications for evaluating the publications of faculty.

1. Comparisons of publishing productivity among faculty are only equitable when made among those who are in similar academic fields and of comparable career age.
2. Comparisons of publication rates are most valid when two or three years are averaged together, rather than using a one-year unit of time or measures of total career productivity.

The trends described in this chapter have several implications for women and minorities. A focus on journal article production as the primary measure of scholarly productivity reflects a "hard" science bias or a bias to those disciplines, such as those in the physical sciences that are characterized by having relative consensus about the central theoretical and research paradigms (Braxton and Bayer 1986). Such a bias advantages faculty in these disciplines, while disadvantaging faculty in other disciplines that are more applied and characterized by a wider diversity of perspectives. Because women and some minorities are concentrated in disciplines characterized as low-consensus or "soft," this has serious implications for how women and some minorities fare in an academic reward structure that relies heavily in quantity of journal articles published. Comparisons of publishing productivity among faculty in a department or program are most equitable when made among those who earned a doctorate in the same field at approximately the same time and from a similar institution.

The second implication for women and minorities in the academic reward structure deals with units of time used to analyze faculty publishing productivity. There are fluctuations in publication patterns among members of the same doctoral cohort that may be attributable to a variety of factors. These may be related to events in the personal life, such as the birth of a child or prolonged illness of parent, or to the nature of the scholarship. Publication may be delayed, for example, for a researcher who tackles a longitudinal study. Also, earlier in this chapter, it was noted that a comparison of career totals of publications are likely to exaggerate gender differences in productivity which tend to expand with time. Comparisons of productivity rates are most reliable when made during comparable points of a person's career, in similar academic fields, and averaging two to three years together to smooth out fluctuations, due to idiosyncracies of the research, or in the personal life.

PUBLISHING PRODUCTIVITY AND
ACADEMIC REWARDS

For the individual faculty member, as well as the university, publication productivity is a central factor in establishing reputation and visibility. One of the long-standing debates in the scholarly literature about faculty productivity is the issue of whether rewards are based on universalistic (scientific merit) or particularistic (selective) criteria. This is the exploration of whether the evidence from the research literature supports one of the four norms of science proposed by Merton (as cited in Braxton 1993) that the academic reward structure is based on universal standards of merit associated primarily with the quality as compared to particularistic criteria, such as gender, race, institutional affiliation, or doctoral origin which are functionally irrelevant to the quality of the output.

The purpose of the second chapter is to review the evidence from the research literature about the relationship between publication productivity and academic rewards and how these vary by gender and race. In this text, *recognition* is used synonymously with the terms, visibility or reputation, and is defined as the formal and informal acknowledgment of the value, originality, impact, or utility of a publication, generally from colleagues external to the institution. Recognition is not an element of the institutional reward structure but an element of the broader, collegial environment. *Reward* is defined as institutional rewards, including tenure, rank, and salary.

Recognition or Visibility

Recognition or visibility is a primary measure of success in science (Fox and Ferri 1992). It is most frequently assessed by measurable indices of accomplishment, such as citations and awards, that reflect the evaluation of peers. These provide an important reinforcement for research and publication, and also are associated with resources. Citations as a measure of the quality of publications is a topic discussed in Chapter 3.

Recognition is established almost exclusively through research and publication, rather than through teaching excellence (Fox 1992). Securing external grant funding is also an element of reputational standing. In most academic areas, reputation is established largely through the publication of articles in professional or academic journals, particularly those considered to be prestigious in the field, and the citations of these articles. Because they are often reprints of "classics" in the field, book chapters were also a significant predictor of

Assessing Faculty Publication Productivity

reputational standing among highly productive social scientists (Davis and Astin 1987). Books contribute to reputation, but carry little weight in the evaluation of many faculty members.

Institutional Rewards

The prominence awarded to scholarly publication in institutional rewards varies by institutional type. Of the respondents to the 1989 National Survey of Faculty (see Table A-1 in Boyer 1990), 83 percent of those at research institutions, 71 percent at doctoral granting institutions, 43 percent at comprehensive institutions, and 24 percent at liberal arts colleges strongly agreed that it is difficult to achieve tenure without publishing. However, the perception that quality and quantity of publications were very important in the departmental reward structure was not significantly associated with a three-year publication rate (Fox 1992).

Gender differences in rank and salary are not fully explained, either by differences in institutional location, or in level of productivity. When compared to men, women-authored papers are less widely read, the payoff in terms of salary is lower, and more publications are required to be promoted (Grant and Ward 1991). They concluded, "Women get less payoff from publishing" (p. 218). Women and men are rewarded differently for career publishing productivity (Nettles and Perna 1995).

Publication Productivity and Rate of Promotion

The promotion rates of African American and Hispanic faculty are lower and Asian American promotion rates are higher than the overall promotion rates for all faculty (Blackburn and Lawrence 1996). Similarly, women's rates of promotion, from associate to full professor, are both lower and slower than men's (Long, Allison, and McGinnis 1993; Ward and Grant 1996). Giving weight to the argument of particularism, gender differences in rank persist even when career age, field, and publication productivity are controlled (Long and Fox 1995; Nettles and Perna, 1995).

Timing issues and differences in what these are interpreted to mean is one of the explanations put forward for gender differences in the rate of promotion. Delay from a traditional time line in completing a doctorate and in entering a full-time faculty position, both have direct effects on the rate of promotion. For example, among academics earning their Ph.D. in biochemistry between 1956-1967, two-thirds of both men and women biochemists delayed entry to a faculty position to pursue a post doctoral fellowship (Long et al. 1993). However, there was a significant *negative* effect for women, and a significant *positive* effect for men, in promotion for a one-year delay from completing a doctorate to entry into a faculty position. Concluding that the negative impact of the delay on promotion was an example of "factors that force equally qualified women to wait longer for promotion" (Long et al. 1993, p. 713), the following is speculated:

> . . . *for women, the negative effect of a delay in the beginning of the academic career may reflect a department's reluctance to promote women who have taken time out from their careers. Men who delay entering the academic market are promoted more rapidly, perhaps to compensate for being "old" assistant professors* (p. 715).

The initial faculty appointment is a second factor that appears to be instrumental in subsequent rewards (Long and Fox 1995). Using a sample of chemists from a similar age cohort, Reskin (1978) found a much higher percentage of women than men had entered an academic career in an untenured position. This is confirmed by more recent data that women are disproportionately more likely than men to be unemployed or in part-time or adjunct positions following the receipt of a doctorate (Dwyer, Flynn, and Inman 1991). A delay in starting a career in a permanent position, carrying the full benefits of a faculty appointment, diminishes the head start and access to resources. These resources are notably influential in the productivity of scholars at the top of their profession who are recognized as prolific.

Publishing Productivity and Salary

Conclusions about the relationship between publishing productivity and salary are not straightforward, because academic rank is one of the strongest predictors of faculty salaries. Also, a significant portion of the gender differences in salaries among academics is related to differences in rank.

Academic rank had the strongest, significant, direct or causal effect on academic salary among nearly 3,000 full-time faculty in four-year colleges and universities. Being female had a significant, direct, negative effect on salary which was not explainable by career age, institutional prestige, discipline, and hours spent a week on teaching and research (Smart 1991). Noting that gender had the largest effects on rank and salary, second only to career age:

> *This singular finding is alarming, for it suggests that faculty members' gender is far more important to their academic rank and salary attainment than the kind of institution which they work, their academic discipline, or the nature of the work they perform in those institutions and disciplines* (Smart 1991, p. 522).

The gender gap in salary is narrowest among the small group of women who are at the highest level of publishing productivity (Fox 1985).

The evidence that gender is a significant predictor of salary—even when level of publishing productivity is controlled—provides further fuel for the argument that particularistic factors have a significant impact on institutional rewards. Additionally, this pattern of reward is so widespread that it cannot be dismissed as being isolated to a few individuals.

Quality and Quantity and Institutional Rewards

Most research literature suggests that institutional rewards, such as tenure, rank, and salary, are influenced more strongly by quantity than quality of publications. In a study of first-named authors of educational research articles, the number of publications for both men and women, was more strongly associated with institutional rewards than the perceived quality of those articles, as judged by a national panel of experts (Persell 1983). Despite finding no significant differences in the judged quality of papers, judged quality was *negatively* associated to an index of rewards for women, but *positively* associated to an index of rewards for men. The relationship was not significant for women, however. Coming to a possibly idiosyncratic conclusion, it is noted that "women doing average or poor research are more likely to have been rewarded than those who do better research" (Persell 1983, p. 45).

Other authors also have suggested that men's and women's publications are held to different standards in promotion. Observing that women's rates of being promoted to associate, as well as to full professor, were lower than comparable men's rates, "women are expected to meet higher standards for promotion" (Long et al. 1993, p. 720). In the process of promotion to full professor, these authors observed that "exceptionally productive women have exceptionally high probabilities of promotion, while the majority of women are less likely than comparable men to be promoted to full professor" (p. 719).

Some of the reasoning for the disparity in rates of promotion can be explained by a lack of agreement about what constitutes quality scholarship. Only 15 percent of the faculty respondents from research, doctoral-granting, and comprehensive institutions strongly agreed with the statement that "most faculty agree on standards of good scholarship" (see Table A-3 in Boyer 1990). The highest levels of agreement were among faculty from the physical sciences and the lowest were in business and the social sciences. Gender and race are more likely to affect rewards in academic areas where there is little or no consensus about what constitutes quality (Long and Fox 1995). In addition, several sources are cited to support the statement that ". . . the more loosely defined and subjective the criteria, the more likely that white men will be perceived as the superior candidates" (Long and Fox 1995, p. 63). Such findings have obvious implications for suggesting the importance of defining clear performance criteria.

The more loosely defined and subjective the criteria, the more likely that white men will be perceived as the superior candidates.

Explanations for Gender Differences in the Impact of Publishing Productivity and Rewards

Work Assignment
Work assignment, particularly the hours per week devoted to research, is one of the factors most strongly associated with publication productivity (Wanner, Lewis, and Gregorio 1981). Time devoted to research and research-related activities, such as obtaining grants and serving on graduate committees, generally enhance productivity, while spending time on tasks not related to research, such as administrative responsibilities, reduces productivity (Nettles and Perna 1995). The highest producers spend about 30 percent of their time on research (Dill 1986). This roughly translates to the equivalent of nearly two full days a week.

Contrary to the idea that they are mutually supportive or that the outstanding researchers are also the outstanding teachers, the demands of research and teaching are competitive (Fox 1992). The relationship between teaching and research may be especially weak for faculty conducting high-status research, such as that appearing in books and journals (Richardson, Parker, and Udell 1992). Faculty members who complete a great deal of publishing spend less time in class, devote fewer hours to preparing for class, and consider teaching less important than research than their colleagues who publish less (Fox 1992).

Work assignment varies by rank, particularly at research institutions. Rank is a factor strongly and directly associated with publishing productivity. The work assignments of senior faculty are more conducive to research productivity because they generally carry smaller teaching loads than junior faculty and are more likely to teach upper-level and graduate courses that have some relationship to their research interests. A much smaller proportion of women than men are at the senior ranks and teaching in graduate programs (Finkelstein 1984). While women and minorities are much more likely than men to have cross-program appointments, little is known about how this affects publishing productivity.

Differences in work assignment and rank, however, do not fully explain gender differences in publishing productivity or institutional rewards. Smart (1991) found that a significant, direct impact of gender on rank and salary persisted even when hours spent on teaching and research were controlled.

Marriage and Children

Even though women academics are much less likely than men academics to be married and they have significantly fewer children (Long et al. 1993), family responsibilities are frequently put forward as an explanation for differences in women's productivity and institutional rewards. The effects of marriage and children on productivity are reported to be statistically insignificant for men.

Table 2.1 is used to summarize research literature spanning almost 20 years about the relationship between marriage and publishing productivity for women.

The majority of findings from the research literature report either no significant effect or a positive effect for married women's publishing productivity (Creamer 1996).

The effects of children on faculty women's publishing productivity are less clear. As shown in Table 2.2, some authors have reported that the presence of children has a significant negative effect on women's publishing productivity,

TABLE 2.1

Summary of Selected Research About the Relationship Between Marriage and Publishing Productivity For Women, By Year

Author(s) (Year)	Significant, Negative	N.S.	Significant, Positive
Astin (1969)	X		
Ferber and Loeb (1973)		X	
Homovitch and Morgenstern (1977)		X	
Reskin (1978)		X	
Astin (1978)		X	
Cole (1979)			X
Helmreich et al. (1980)		X	
Astin and Davis (1985)			X
Fox and Faver (1985)	X		
Dupagne (1993)			X

while others have documented no significant effect, or a significant positive effect.

While responsibility for young children has been pointed to as a reason for women's late entry into faculty positions and starting a publishing career, several authors have suggested that a positive relationship between marriage and productivity may be related to married women having greater access than single women to mentors and colleagues (Astin and Davis 1985; Long 1990). The issue about marriage most related to productivity is one of career continuity (Reskin 1978). Delayed entry to a faculty position may help to explain the finding that academic women's productivity tends to peak later than men's (Astin and Davis 1985; Kyvik 1990; Toren 1991).

Summary

This chapter has presented a summary of some of the information available about the relationship between recognition, institutional rewards, and publishing productivity and how

Table 2.2

Summary of Selected Research About the Relationship Between Children and Publishing Productivity For Women, By Year

Author(s) (Year)	Significant, Negative	N.S.	Significant, Positive
Ferber and Loeb (1973)		X	
Homovitch and Morgenstern (1977)		X	
Reskin (1978)		X	
Hargens et al. (1978)	X		
Helmreich et al. (1980)		X	
Fox and Faver (1985)			X
Cole and Zuckerman (1987)		X	
Kyvik (1990)			X
Toren (1991)			X
Dupagne (1993)	X		

these vary by gender. Although it is known that women and minorities are under-represented at prestigious institutions and at the senior academic ranks, and over-represented in less prestigious institutions and at the junior ranks, there is almost no research available about the relationship between race, publication productivity and these factors. When taken as a whole, the findings reported in this chapter strongly suggest that particularism, rather than universalism, has typically operated in institutional reward structures.

Key points raised in this chapter are:

1. Recognition or visibility is almost exclusively established through scholarly publications, rather than excellence in teaching.
2. The number of journal articles published is a significant predictor of reputation, visibility, and institutional rewards, such as academic rank and salary.

3. Quantity of publications is more strongly associated than quality of publications with institutional rewards.
4. Gender differences in rank, salary, promotion, and time required for promotion are only partially explained by differences in publication productivity.
5. Differences in work assignment and rank explain some of the gender differences in career productivity.
6. Career delays and interruptions have a long-term impact on career publication productivity.

Implications for Practice

It would take a far more substantial review of the literature than has been presented in this chapter to explain gender and race differences in the academic reward structure. Although it skirts the larger question of the validity of publishing productivity as a primary index of faculty productivity (noted in subsequent chapters), the finding that men and women academics with comparable publication records generally are not comparably rewarded, raises puzzling questions. These questions focus on the academic reward system and the role that non-merit based criteria, such as gender and race, play in it.

Major implications for practice raised by this chapter are:

1. Initial appointments to anything other than tenure track faculty positions may have substantial, long-term consequences for publishing productivity, particularly for women and minorities.
2. Clearly defined performance criteria are important in all academic fields, but they are especially important in fields where there is little consensus about what constitutes good scholarship.
3. Institutional processes and policies do not necessarily affect men's and women's publishing productivity in the same way. Because of a lack of external recognition, institutional rewards and reinforcement have a greater long-term impact on women's publishing level than on men's.
4. Teaching and research are competing demands. Time devoted to research is strongly associated with publishing productivity. When publication productivity is a performance expectation, work assignments must be shaped to present the opportunity to devote high quality time to research.

Initial appointments to anything other than tenure track faculty positions may have substantial, long-term consequences for publishing productivity, particularly for women and minorities.

5. While women with extraordinary publication records may actually have a greater chance of promotion than comparable men, the bigger challenge for faculty review committees is to ensure that women with average publication records are not held to a higher standard than comparable men.

Initial appointments to anything other than tenure track faculty positions may have substantial, long-term consequences for publishing productivity, particularly for women and minorities. While more institutions are developing so-called family-friendly policies that allow for stopping the tenure clock for such events as childbirth or adoption, these do not circumvent a pervasive work ideology that interprets such interruptions as an indication that a faculty member is less than fully committed or serious about her career, making women reluctant to utilize them. Similarly, it does not address a traditional ideology about family, suggesting that work and family are incompatible for women; this may help us to understand why the proportion of married faculty women continues to be significantly lower than the proportion of married faculty men.

ASSESSING PUBLISHING PERFORMANCE

This chapter extends the discussion of an issue raised in the previous chapter by examining the question of whether commonly utilized indices of the quantity and quality of publishing productivity are accurate reflections of merit, that are applied uniformly, or whether they are influenced by particularistic factors, such as gender and race.

Citations are often used by colleges and universities as a measure of quality of research in tenure, promotion, and salary decisions (Ward and Grant 1996). The term "citation" refers to publications that appear in the reference list of a scholarly publication. These generally refer to references that are indexed in the publications, including on-line and electronic databases, of the Institute for Scientific Information (ISI). Citation indexes are available in most academic disciplines, including the arts and humanities, social sciences, and sciences. For each discipline, ISI produces a source index, listing by author and co-author(s) the complete reference list of each article published in journals that are indexed by ISI, by year. It also produces a citation index, listing the lead author of journal articles who have been cited, as well as an index of classics that are the most cited publications in a field. Books and book chapters are not indexed by ISI, except as in the source index. It is estimated that only about 10 percent to 25 percent of journal articles are indexed (Mooney 1991). The indices produced by ISI can be used to count the number of times a journal article, authored by an individual, has been cited in a given year.

In addition to its use as a measure of faculty publishing productivity, citations also are used for ranking the quality, as measured by the relative productivity of faculty, of academic departments and institutions, including the assessment of the quality and impact of journals. A full review of the uses of citations, other than in relation to its use as a measure of faculty publishing productivity, is not within the scope of this chapter.

Measuring Quantity of Publications

Two measures are commonly utilized in the research literature to assess the level of publication productivity. The most frequent measure is a straightforward count of the number of publications. Most publication counts rely on number of journal articles, partly because of the ease of measuring them. The source index produced by ISI can be used to count the number of publications in journals indexed by ISI in any given year. These counts are sometimes weighted by the impact of the journal, as reported by ISI, based on the average citation rate of articles in that journal. Although relatively easy to calculate, simple counts of the number of journal articles fail to account for variations in the type, length, and quality of articles appearing in journals. They encourage an emphasis on quantity of publications, rather than quality. There are great variations in the standard length of articles across academic fields. It is not possible to use ISI to get a count of the number of publications, other than in journal articles appearing in a limited number of indexed journals.

A second way that publication productivity is assessed is through weighted counts. These generally consider a number of different types of publications which are awarded numerical weights, based on a judgment by experts of their contribution to knowledge. Such schemes often distinguish between different types of books (edited books, textbooks, monographs, manuals, etc.) and articles, which may take the form of full-length, research-based articles; literature reviews; commentaries; book reviews, or brief research notes. Some of these weighting schemes adjust for differences in length of publications. These systems generally categorize a publication by the type of source it appears in, rather than by a judgment about the actual content of the publication.

The weights awarded to different types of publications are not standardized and vary by publication. For example, Garland (1990) calculated a normalized weighted score to account for the productivity of library and information faculty during a five year period. She awarded six points for a monograph, four points for a textbook, and two points for an article or book chapter to create a sum which was the weighted score. This was then divided by five to reach a yearly weighted score. Points were divided among the authors of co-authored publications.

While the scholarly contribution of books is devalued in many academic fields, particularly in some high-consensus fields where they are not viewed as the place to go to find cutting-edge material, a review of the weighting systems, reported in eight articles, found that original scholarly books and monographs were weighted more heavily than journal articles. However, the importance of developing weighting systems that are adjusted for disciplinary differences is strongly urged (Braxton and Bayer 1986).

In order to assess the full range of faculty member's contribution to knowledge, it is proposed that some unpublished documents, such as papers presented at conferences, and technical reports produced for funding agencies, should be considered in productivity measures that assess different types of publications (Braxton and Bayer 1986). Types of publications, other than journal articles, such as book chapters and review articles, may be better indicators of national visibility and collegial recognition (Astin 1991).

Citations as a Measure of Quality

As with judgments made in the institutional reward structure, peers or colleagues within and outside of the institution play a central role judging a faculty member's scholarly output. The primary, traditional index of quality is the usefulness of a work to the extent that it contributes to knowledge, rather than to practice. Usefulness means the extent that it becomes the "basis for further work by other scientists" (Becher 1989, p. 59). This perspective recognizes a fairly narrow audience for most scholarly publications. There are other scholars who, by virtue of sharing an expertise in the same area, are the most equipped to judge the merits. It also reinforces the focus in most academic areas on measuring quality through the citation of journal articles which is, again, a practice restricted largely to the academic community.

Citations of an individual's work are said to reflect a number of different things, including quality, quantity, impact, collegial networks, and visibility or reputation (Toutkoushian 1994). Attributing a similar broad band of ways that citations measure both the quantity and quality of publication productivity, ". . . citation counts provide an objective measure of productivity, significance, quality, utility, influence, effectiveness, or impact of a scholar and his or her scholarly products" (Braxton and Bayer 1986, p. 35). Only a small percentage of cites refer to a publication in a negative or critical way (Lutz 1990).

Citations are considered a measure of quality by virtue of providing a way to measure the *impact or usefulness* of the work, as reflected in the number of other scholars who refer to the work in their publications. The length of time it took for an idea to be disseminated can be calculated by the number of years until citations peak. Average age of citations are sometimes used to determine which journals are publishing cutting edge or "research front" as compared to "archival" material (Budd 1990).

Citations also are used to identify *research networks* or the linkages among scholars (Braxton and Bayer 1986). Citations can be a "proxy" for "lines of intellectual exchange" (Grant and Ward 1991, p. 217). This provides a measure of how widely a piece of scholarly work has been disseminated, as well as visibility and recognition in the academic community. A broad range of references to a publication by authors, in a variety of journals, demonstrates professional ties outside an area of specialty (Becher 1989). Citations are a social practice that "legitimizes the voice of the cited author" (Lutz 1990, p. 611). Since only a small proportion of journals are indexed, and these are most likely to be relatively mainstream journals, an additional source of bias can be introduced by relying on readily available sources of citations to measure research networks.

In addition to providing a convenient way to measure different dimensions of quality, citations also serve to reinforce publishing, particularly among the small group of authors who are frequently cited. Citations are viewed as "a form of symbolic capital" (Lutz 1990, p. 611), because of their association to visibility and status, such as when a piece of scholarly work is recognized as being among the classics. It is suggested that gender differences of reinforcement provide one explanation for gender differences in scholarly productivity (Astin 1991). Also, it is proposed that citations are particularly instrumental to the productivity of academics who lack other rewards, due to their gender or position (Reskin 1978). The idea that women may receive less recognition for publishing productivity is pursued further in the next chapter.

Characteristics of Citation Patterns

Citation Rates

The average citation rates of a journal article are quite low. Most journal articles are cited either no times or one time (Braxton and Bayer 1986). About 22 percent of the scientific articles indexed by ISI were united during the five-year period following its publication (Mooney 1991). Seventy percent of the articles in the Science Citation Index were cited once, and less than nine articles out of a thousand were cited more than 100 times (Long and Fox 1995).

Relationship between quantity and quality. Quantity of publications and quantity of citations are highly correlated (Cole and Zuckerman 1984), suggesting that quantity of publications has a significant impact on quality, as measured by citations. For instance, a strong, positive correlation between quantity of articles and citation counts ranging from .81 to .93 are found across the careers of a doctoral cohort of biochemists (Long 1992). Those with the largest number of publications in peer reviewed journals are those with the greatest number of lifetime citations.

Self Citations
The rate of self-citation is high enough that it is fairly common practice to remove self-citations from total citation accounts. Prolific publishers can have the strongest impact on their citation rates through self-citations. Self-citations account for 10 to 20 percent of the total citations received for a published article (Smart and Bayer 1986). Similarly, it is calculated that 7.5 percent of the citations in articles, in four journals of anthropology were self-citations, and that male authors made significantly more self citations than did female authors (Lutz 1990).

Age of Citations
More than 60 percent of all publications appearing in the reference list of articles in three core journals in higher educations were more than five years old (Budd 1990). The average age of materials cited in these journals varied by type of publication and ranged from an average age of 9.09 years for a book chapter, to 9.36 years for a journal article, and 11.69 years for a book (p. 88). Average age of citations vary by academic field and among sub-specialty areas because of variation in journal acceptance rates (Braxton and Bayer 1986). It is shorter in the natural and physical sciences, where articles generally are recognized more rapidly through citations, than in the social sciences and humanities (Budd 1990).

The average age of citations appearing in the reference list of an article reflects, in part, the time lag required for publication, while also being an indication of the number of people publishing, without respect to a given topic. Articles on nonmainstream topics may receive few citations simply because few people are publishing on the topic. Since most publications cited in articles referenced in ISI are greater than five years, citations are more likely to be a consideration in promotion, from associate to full professor, than in the decision to award tenure and promote to associate professor, which occurs in the traditional, six-year time frame.

Highly Cited Authors

For both men and women, only a small number of scholars are highly cited (Cole and Zuckerman 1984). Highly cited authors are primarily those who have appeared as the senior or sole authors of a large number of journal articles, rather than scholars who have produced one or two widely read books, partly because of the way citations are counted. There is only a modest, positive correlation between total article and book publication (Blackburn, Behymer, and Hall 1978).

As with prolific authors, the most cited scholars in a field are almost exclusively white males. Examples of this, from two different academic fields, are provided in Table 3.1, reproduced from Budd (1990), and Table 3.2, reproduced from Liebowitz and Palmer (1988). Similar information is published in other academic fields (e.g., Radhakrishna and Jackson 1995, in agricultural education; Thomas and Kenzie 1986, in marital and family therapy). For both articles, in which findings are displayed in the tables, the original source of the information listed only initials. The author used the *National Faculty Directory* from a number of years to identify the first name. No comment was made by the authors of either article about the total absence of women from the lists of most cited authors in the fields.

Table 3.1, reproduced from Budd (1990) with first names added, reflects only senior or sole authors cited in articles in three core journals in higher education over a six-year period, from 1982-1987. The complete lack of women's names on the list is not representative of women on the faculty in education, or of women publishing in these journals. In 1984, 36 percent of the faculty in education were women (Ransom 1990), and 15 percent of the faculty in programs in higher education were women (Newell and Kuh 1989). During a five-year period between 1987 and 1991, 36.3 percent of the senior or sole authors in the same three core journals in higher education were women (Creamer 1994).

As with prolific authors, the most cited scholars in a field are almost exclusively white males.

Table 3.1

Ten Most Cited Authors in Higher Education*

Rank	Author
1.	Alexander W. Astin
2.	Ernest T. Pascarella
3.	John A. Centra
4.	J. Victor Baldridge
5.	Kenneth A. Feldmman
6.	Vincent Tinto
7.	Herbert W. Marsh
8.	Jeffrey Pfeffer
9.	Burton R. Clark
10a.	Anthony Biglan
10b.	Peter M. Blau

*Excludes self-citations. Source: John M. Budd (1990). Higher education literature: Characteristics of citation patterns. *Journal of Higher Education*, 61, p. 94. First names added by the author from information supplied in the *National Faculty Directory*, 1976-1996.

Table 3.2

Ten Most Cited Authors in Economics*

Rank	Author
1.	Martin S. Feldstein
2.	Kenneth J. Arrow
3.	Paul A. Samuelson
4.	Robert J. Barro
5.	Gary S. Becker
6.	Robert E. Lucas
7.	Eugene F. Famma
8.	Henri Theil
9.	George Stigler
10.	Thomas J. Sargent

*Excludes self-citations. As listed in S. J. Liebowitz and J. P. Palmer (1988). Reviewing assessments of economics departments. *Quarterly Review of Economics and Business*, 28, p. 108. First names added by the author from information supplied in the *National Faculty Directory*, 1976-1996.

In a second example, from another academic field, the top 10 publishers in economics for the four-year period of 1978 to 1981 are shown in Table 3.2, as reprinted from Liebowitz and Palmer (1988). Once again, no women's names appear on the list. The Committee on the Status of Women in the

Economics Profession (1980) reported there were less than 100 women on the faculty in departments awarding doctoral degrees in economics. A study of the citation patterns of journals in economics (Ferber 1986, 1988) noted that during 1982-1983, 9.7 percent of the articles in labor economics and 3.7 percent of the articles in financial economics were written by one or more women. This suggests that, although the number might be small, a few women's names would be expected on the list of top publishers in economics.

Explanations for why so few women appear on lists of highly cited authors correspond in many ways with the explanations provided in the first chapter of why so few women are among prolific publishers. One of the major reasons that men are cited more than women is because they publish more (Cole and Zuckerman 1984; Creswell 1985) and because women are over-represented among nonpublishers and under-represented among prolific publishers (Long 1992).

Gender and Measures of Publishing Productivity

A number of questions have been raised in the research literature about the role of gender in evaluating the quality and quantity of publications. They include whether articles by male authors are cited significantly more frequently than those by female authors, and if work by women is more likely than work by men to appear in less prestigious journals. All of these issues have significant implications for career advancement for academics, particularly those in institutions where research and publication is central to the reward structure.

Gender and Citation Rates

There is little disagreement that the majority of citations supplied in any given article, whether it's a male or female author, are given to publications authored by men. For instance, in looking at citation patterns in an equal number of male- and female-authored articles in five disciplines, 98 percent of the citations in math, 96 percent in finance, 89 percent in labor economics, 86 percent in sociology, and 67 percent in developmental psychology involved publications authored by men (Ferber 1988, p. 85).

Gender differences in citation rates become insignificant when the number of publications are controlled (Davis and Astin 1987; Long 1990; Ward, Gast, and Grant 1992). On the other hand, Lutz (1990) determined that female anthropologists produced about one-fourth of the publications during the time period studied but only received about one-fifth of the citations. Prolific women in one academic field, biochemistry, although very few in number, received more average citations per article, per career than their male colleagues (Long 1990, 1992). For both men and women, citation rates and patterns vary by level of productivity.

Women as senior authors. Citation indexes attribute all citations to the first or solo author, known as the senior author. In some academic fields, the first-named author in a list that is not arranged alphabetically is the one who is assumed to have taken the lead in conceptualizing the article. In other academic fields, such as in the physical sciences, the lead author may simply be the principal investigator who "owns" the data, so to speak, because it comes from research conducted in his or her laboratory. In other fields, the lead author is generally recognized as the person whose name appears last in the list of authors. While such traditional citing conventions deflate everyone's publication record, the impact is disproportionately large for women because they are much less likely than men to appear as senior author.

Table 3.3

Summary of Selected Research About the Percentage of Women Appearing in Journals as Senior Author, By Area and Year

Area (No. of Journals)	Year(s)	Percentage of Women	Source (Year)
Psychology (14)	1982	25.04	White (1985)
Higher education (8)	1975-1981	16.30	Silverman (1987)
Higher education (4)	1987-1991	36.26	Creamer (1994)
Sociology (10)	1974-1983	21.00	Ward and Grant (1985)
Business (27)	1962-1984	15.1	Walter, Fry, and Chaisson (1990)

Table 3.3 summarizes the findings of selected studies published in 1985 and after, regarding the proportion of women appearing as senior authors in journals in a number of academic areas. The proportion of women appearing as the senior author of articles is increasing in most journals (Ward and Grant 1985). The rate women are cited is directly related to how frequently, or infrequently, they appear as senior author.

Same-sex citation patterns. Part of the gender differences in citation patterns are explained by the relatively consistent finding that both men and women have a penchant for citing authors of their same sex (Ferber 1986, 1988; Ward et al. 1992; Ward and Grant 1996). Women are significantly more likely than men to cite female authors (Ferber 1988). In journal articles in anthropology, which is characterized as one of the least male dominated disciplines, women cited other women about twice as often as men (Lutz 1990).

A similar pattern of same-sex preference has been observed in manuscript acceptance rates. A number of studies have replicated the finding that when an identical manuscript was attributed to a male and to a female author, the manuscript supposedly authored by a woman was accepted significantly more often by female than by male reviewers (Lloyd 1990). The under-representation of women as editors or members of the editorial boards of journals is said to contribute to the low proportion of articles that appear in most journals that list a woman as the senior author (Nicoloff and Forrest 1988; White 1984, 1985).

The practice of same-sex citing reflects patterns of intellectual exchange and collegial networks that are gender segregated (Ward and Grant 1996). It is likely that the same pattern holds true by race. Same-sex citing reflects differences in the topics of men's and women's writing, whether the work is considered mainstream or nonmainstream, and whether it is indexed in widely available sources. Women's scholarship may largely be reaching a female audience:

> "... there is substantial evidence that women's scholarship might be delimited in impact, reaching audiences that are primarily female" (Ward and Grant 1996, p. 197).

Women in nontraditional disciplines or in academic fields where the proportion of women publishers is small, are among the least likely to be cited. These are the same group of women who are likely to be doubly disadvantaged by the pattern of same-sex citing (Ferber 1988). The proclivity of women to cite women may ultimately advantage women in academic areas that are female dominated.

Prestige of journals. An additional issue raised in the discussion about gender differences in citation patterns, is the prestige of journals, as generally assessed by impact of the journal or the extent that the average article in that journal is cited. While finding no gender differences in the proportion of articles authored by women in journals of prestige (Lutz 1990), others have observed that the articles of female authors are concentrated in less prestigious journals (Walters, Fry, and Chaisson 1990) and interdisciplinary journals (Ward et al. 1992).

Another way to look at the prestige of the publications of women, or the impact of their scholarship, is through citation classics, or works that are reprinted as classics in a field. Several studies have documented the lack of representation of female authors on lists of "canon-setting" works that often appear on the reading lists of graduate courses (Lutz 1990). For example, of 85 reviews of classics in the field of anthropology, only one was authored by a woman (Lutz, 1990). In another study, no works, authored or co-authored, by someone with a woman's name appeared in the list of 20 most cited books in three core journals in higher education (Budd 1990). In a study of citation classics from *Current Contents,* a publication of ISI which features essays by authors of highly cited articles, in areas of research selected by the editors, a comparison of men's publications versus women's publications, revealed that a significantly higher percentage of recognized citation classics were books (Astin 1991). Although Astin did not suggest this, it seems that it takes a more substantial publication for women to be recognized as a scientific authority.

Several stylistic conventions of the citation indices produced by ISI may lead to the underestimation of an individual's publishing productivity.

Critique of Citations

Several stylistic conventions of the citation indices produced by ISI may lead to the underestimation of an individual's publishing productivity. A major factor is that the majority of journals are not indexed by ISI. In addition: (a) only first or sole authors are indexed, so that all citations of a work are attributed to the first or sole authors; (b) only initials and surnames are used, which may cause confusion among people who have changed names, or who have the same last name; (c) only journal articles in a small percent of peer reviewed journals are indexed, and (d) there is no adjustment for self-citations (Braxton and Bayer 1986). Citing conventions may have a disproportionate impact on women who publish—when compared to men, women are (a) less likely to be the primary, first, or sole author of a journal article; (b) more likely to have changed their name; (c) less likely to publish in prestigious journals, and (d) less likely to cite themselves.

In addition to articles published in journals, other types of publications contribute to the communication of knowledge, and to an individual's national reputation and prestige. Books, book chapters, and review articles that provide a synthesis and analysis of the literature on a topic also enhance visibility (Astin 1991; Davis and Astin 1987). In many fields, however, books, particularly those suspected of having popular appeal, are devalued in the process of institutional personnel decisions. Unpublished research outcomes, such as those distributed among colleagues at professional meetings or invited conferences, represent the real "cutting edge" of research, rather than journal articles which take years to produce, publish, and reach peak citations. Preprints are common in certain specialized academic areas where results of research are shared among a "privileged" network before publication (Becher 1989, p. 81). Women who submit proposals for programs at professional meetings are at a comparable, or higher rate than men, but they may be less likely to follow through to publication (Lutz 1990).

Summary

The third chapter was used to review traditional measures of the quality and quantity of scholarly publications, and how the implications of such measures vary by gender. Because of their role in institutional reward structures, traditional measures of faculty publishing productivity have significant implications for career advancement among academics. Key points raised in this chapter are:

1. Citations are often used to measure quality of research in tenure, promotion, and salary decisions, particularly at doctoral institutions where research and publishing are central elements of the institutional reward structure.

2. In the research literature, publishing productivity is most commonly measured through a count of publications or through counts that are weighted by type of publication. The weight awarded different types of publication vary by discipline and to what extent the publication is considered central to knowledge dissemination.
3. Peers, particularly those who share expertise in a research topic, play a central role in judging the quality of scholarship.
4. Citations measure publishing productivity by reflecting the extent and breadth of utilization by peers of an article published in a small number of peer reviewed journals.
5. Most journal articles receive few, if any, citations. Only a very small percentage of faculty are highly cited, and these are almost exclusively white males.
6. Quantity of publications and rate of citation are highly related. The most cited authors are generally those who have produced a large number of journal articles.
7. The majority of citations in most journal are to works authored by men.
8. Women generally receive less visibility or recognition for their publications. They are cited less than men, partly because they publish less, partly because they are less likely to cite themselves, and partly because they are more likely than men to publish on topics considered to be outside the mainstream.
9. Both men and women, but particularly women, tend to cite authors of the same sex.

Implications for Practice

Traditional measures of quantity and quality of publication productivity rely on what we can easily measure, and it can be shown as an example of how our evaluation strategies tend to rely on what we can measure. Citations offer the advantage of convenience of access, standardization across academic fields, and reliability.

Being quantifiable does not necessarily equate with being nonbiased. One reason that feminists bristle at the use of the expression "academic standards" is the doubt that the same criteria are used similarly to judge the products of the work of women and minorities, coupled with a suspicion that criteria may have been designed in ways that are most likely to advantage certain groups. The virtual absence of women authors from the lists of the most prolific authors, the most cited authors, and the authors of works considered to be classics in a field, may be interpreted as a reflection of less ability, or less interest, or as a product of a system that consistently serves to limit a small, homogenous group for reward.

Major implications for strategies to evaluate faculty publishing productivity are:

1. The length of time it takes to become cited, and the low average number of citations per article, suggest that citations, as a measure of quality, are unlikely to be relevant in tenure decisions for most faculty.

2. Given the citing conventions that attribute all cites to the lead author, reliance on citation counts from indexed sources devalues collaboration and underestimates publication level. This has an especially negative impact on the evaluation of women's credentials because of the frequency with which they appear as second or co-author. This can be offset somewhat by asking the candidate to manually adjust figures to reflect citations of co-authored papers.

3. Citations emphasize communication among academics in the same specialized domain and provide little insight of the applicability to practitioners or nonacademics. Evidence of the breadth of knowledge dissemination can be better assessed by considering a wider audience, such as invited speeches or evidence that publications are used in graduate instruction.

4. Since they reflect collegial networks, scholars are probably aware of some of the people who are citing them. Candidates can be asked to supply information in their portfolios about who is citing them, as well as citations in unpublished sources, or sources not documented in ISI.

5. Since citation rates are so influenced by level of productivity, total numbers of citations should not be used to compare the productivity of individuals. Having a journal article with more than one citation should be considered very unusual.

6. Given that citation patterns and rates vary by discipline, and depend on such things as journal acceptance rates, including the cohesiveness of networks of collegial ex-

change, they should not be used as the solitary criterion for institutional rewards, particularly in comparisons of faculty in different academic areas or subspecialties. Recognition through awards, conference proposals, successful grant applications, invitations to participate in panels and invited conferences, and invitations to serve as a peer reviewer for grant proposals are a few other indicators of professional esteem.

7. A broad range of types of publications contribute to dissemination of knowledge in a field, particularly when the audience is extended to consider graduate students and practitioners in a field. Judgments about publication productivity should evaluate the contribution of all types of publications, including journal articles, book review, essays, books, book chapters, reviews, and unpublished documents circulated among colleagues. Candidates can be asked to supply evidence of contributions to knowledge in their fields, in their portfolio.

"Reward systems that fail to honor excellence often produce social conditions that lead to deviance" (Cole and Cole 1973, p. 15). One reason for faculty alienation is a belief that particularism, rather than universalism, impacts academic rewards (Braxton 1993). Evidence that traditional measures of publishing productivity are applied differently, depending on the race or gender of the faculty member being evaluated, suggests that something other than scholarly excellence is being honored. This may provide one reason why members of marginalized groups often express skepticism about traditional measures of publishing productivity. When the so-called objective measures of faculty productivity serve to advantage one group of scholars and disadvantage another, it is absolutely essential to challenge the value of the criteria themselves.

CONCEPTUAL EXPLANATIONS FOR GENDER DIFFERENCES IN PUBLISHING PRODUCTIVITY

Despite its emergence in the 1970s as a major stream in the research literature about scholarly productivity, only a few, comprehensive reviews of the literature are available that present conceptual explanations for gender differences in faculty publishing productivity. Dwyer, Flynn, and Inman (1991) and Ward and Grant (1996) provide two exceptions to this statement. These are distinguished from other reviews of the literature, such as by Fox (1985), that analyze correlates of faculty publishing productivity without exploring in detail how these vary by gender. Fox (1995) and Sonnert and Holton (1995a, 1995b) summarize individual and environmental factors associated with aspects of career attainment in science, such as rank, location, and rewards.

The chapter is used to summarize the conceptual explanations offered in the research literature to explain the gender gap in publication productivity. While often not significant, when short periods of time are utilized, apparent gender differences emerge when cumulative, career productivity is analyzed (Cole and Singer 1991). This chapter is organized around the basic proposition that gender, and, probably race or ethnicity, influence publishing productivity indirectly through the four, key variables that operate in a highly interactive way: resources, recognition, reward, and reinforcement. The purpose of this chapter is not to provide an exhaustive scholarly analysis or critique of the research literature but to highlight the elements of the explanations with the most direct implication for academics in a position to judge the publishing credentials of faculty. The chapter closes with a discussion of the implications for the evaluation of faculty publishing credentials.

As illustrated by the three tables that appear at the end of this chapter, conceptual explanations for gender-related correlates of faculty publishing productivity can be organized into three main factors: individual factors, institutional factors, and environmental factors. Individual factors highlight characteristics of the individual producer as being central to explaining gender differences in publishing productivity. Institutional factors point to characteristics of the department and institution where the faculty member earned his or her degree, and is employed, as central to understanding gender differences in publishing productivity. Environmental factors point to characteristics external to the institution, as being the most instrumental to understanding gender differences in publishing productivity.

Distinctions are made in the use of some terms in this chapter which are frequently used interchangeably in the literature. *Reward* designates institutional rewards, such as salary, promotion, and tenure. *Resources* is the quality and quantity of institutional and external resources, including the opportunity offered by training and employment in a prestigious institution or department and work assignment. *Recognition* is used synonymously with visibility and reputation and is defined as formal and informal acknowledgment of the value, impact, utility, or originality of a person's work. Gender differences in the operation of recognition and reward were discussed in previous chapters. *Reinforcement* refers to formal and informal feedback from colleagues.

Among others, Astin (1984), and Blackburn and Lawrence (1996) presented psychosocial models of faculty productivity that are not included in these tables because they explain faculty performance in general, rather than the narrower aspect of faculty performance, publishing productivity, which is the topic of this monograph. These models are not offered to explain gender differences in productivity.

Individual Characteristics

There is little doubt that several individual characteristics, such as ability and interest in research, are strongly associated with publishing productivity. Explanations offered in the research literature, which relate to personal qualities and explain gender differences in publishing productivity, are summarized in Table 4.1.

Most of the recent literature points to a growing convergence in the interests and habits of male and female academics. No significant gender differences have been reported in men's and women's commitment to research and publication (Bean and Kuh 1988), ability (Long and Fox 1995), motivation (Fox and Faver 1985), or attitudes and practices related to productivity (Fox and Faver 1985). Individual characteristics account for little in explaining women's lower success in science (Fox 1995). Percentage of time devoted to research is a strong predictor of publishing productivity (Blackburn, Wenzel, and Bieber 1994). When examined in the aggregate across all types of institutions, female faculty spend more time on teaching, particularly undergraduate

Table 4.1

Major Conceptual Explanations for Gender Differences in the Individual Factors Associated With Publishing Productivity

Variables	Explanation (Source(s))
Time Devoted to Research	Women faculty spend more time on teaching and devote less time to research than men faculty (Finkelstein 1984).
Perceptions of Authority	Gender is not a significant predictor of publishing productivity when perceptions of self competence are assessed (Blackburn, Bieber, Lawrence, and Trautvetter 1991). Particularly for faculty women in the junior ranks, establishing a sense of authority interferes with women's productivity (Kirsch 1993).

teaching, and dedicate less time to research than male faculty (Finkelstein 1984). Some authors interpret these findings to suggest that female faculty have a greater interest in or preference for teaching than male faculty. Occupational segregation of women in disciplines and institutions with a stronger teaching and service mission, and the impact this has on work assignment, offers a more likely explanation on why female faculty, in general, devote less time than male faculty to research. While individual qualities cannot be overlooked, they present an oversimplified picture of what it takes to be productive as a scholarly writer. Productivity is the product of the interaction of individual qualities and environmental conditions (Astin 1984; Blackburn and Lawrence 1996). Additionally, others have suggested that a faculty member's perception of institutional expectations, along with self assessment of competence, influences how they allocate their time and how long they persist at a task. A woman's career choice and work behavior are influenced by an assessment of the available opportunities (Astin 1984).

The issue of perception of self competence can also be interpreted in the comments of some feminist authors who have explored the experiences of women academics and their struggle to internalize an identity as an authority, or to develop their own voice. Women's so-called lack of self confidence arises, not from lack of ability, but from their "professional vulnerability" (Aisenberg and Harrington 1988, p. 67), due to marginalized positions and from social norms "dictating the impropriety of an authoritative voice for women" (p. 69). In Gesa Kirsch's book, *Women Writing the Academy: Audience, Authority, and Transformation* (1993), which focuses on the experiences of some successful women academic writers, the following observation was made about the issue of establishing voice:

> *Scholars in women's studies have argued that establishing authority is further complicated for women—as well as for other groups historically marginalized in institutions like the university—because part of having author-ity entails being perceived as an authority* (p. 49).

It is further observed that this struggle was least pronounced among women faculty in the senior ranks with extensive publication records. Presumably, these are women with more secure positions who have achieved some level of recognition among their colleagues. She noted, ". . . the more years of experiences writers had, the more confidence they expressed in their writing ability and the more authority they assumed" (p. 51).

Institutional Factors

Reward

The relationship between institutional rewards, such as salary and promotion, and publishing productivity was discussed in Chapter 2. Institutional rewards include salary, promotion, and tenure, as well as informal and formal communication about the expectation for research and its association with rewards. Institutional factors that explain gender differences in publishing productivity are summarized in Table 4.2.

Since the strength of the relationship between publishing productivity and institutional rewards is not as strong for women as for men, differences in the impact of institutional rewards has been offered as one explanation for gender differences in publishing productivity. Institutional rewards and climate are more influential to women's long term productivity than to men's, because they are less likely than majority men to benefit from the resources, rewards, and reinforcement that accrue from recognition or visibility from colleagues external to the institution (Long and Fox 1995; Reskin 1978).

Women's so-called lack of self confidence arises, not from lack of ability, but from their "professional vulnerability" due to marginalized positions and from social norms "dictating the impropriety of an authoritative voice for women."

TABLE 4.2

Major Conceptual Explanations for Gender Differences in the Institutional Factors Associated With Publishing Productivity

Variables	Explanation (Source(s))
Reward	When compared to men with comparable publishing records, women get fewer institutional rewards in the form of rates of promotion, speed of promotion, and salaried groups (Long and Fox 1995; Reskin 1978). Many faculty women are distinguished by their reluctance to "play by the rules" of the academic reward structure (Aisenberg and Harrington 1988).
Resources	Lack of access to institutional resources limits the amount of time many women faculty have to devote to research and publication, and to participate in influential collegial networks (Long 1990).

On the subject of faculty women, particularly in science, a number of authors have used the metaphor of women as outsiders in the academic community. For example, Zuckerman, Cole, and Bruer (1991) referred to women as being in "the outer circle" in the title of their text.

Aisenberg and Harrington (1988) used a similar metaphor in their book title. Offering one viewpoint about women's interpretation of the institutional rewards, they borrowed on language coined by Patricia Hill Collins (1986), a sociologist: One commonality among the experience of female academics was the stance of an "informed outsider" (p. 86). Also, they associated the standpoint of the outsider, which is characterized by "the dual perspective of close knowledge and psychological distance" (p. 86) of the social system, with ". . . the examination of familiar subjects critically, from an angle of visions that differs from prevailing authorities" (p. 86). Rather than a lack of knowledge about institutional and structural elements associated with productivity, the women they studied voiced an extreme reluctance to play by the "rules of the game." It is their interpretation that resistance distinguishes many faculty women, not inadequate or incomplete socialization to the norms and values of the academic work place. The mistrust of formal authority is an understandable by-product of an academic reward structure that doesn't appear to equally reward faculty.

Resources

Resources have been defined as "access to the means of production" (Cole and Zuckerman 1984). This includes resources afforded by institutional location, such as work assignment; examples are teaching load, as well as committee and service assignments. Access to clerical support, laboratory assistants, graduate students, and postdoctoral fellows are other examples of resources, and also physical resources, such as equipment and laboratory space that are necessary for research. These have a profound impact on both the ability to dedicate time to scholarship, as well as provide the tools to conduct it. Resources include those that support collegial relationships central to reward, recognition, and reinforcement. Sociodemographic variables, such as gender and ethnicity, influence faculty performance indirectly "by limiting or enhancing one's access to resources and opportunities" (Blackburn Lawrence 1996, p. 16).

The research literature consistently supports a strong relationship between institutional location and publishing productivity. The prestige of both the institution where doctoral training was received, and the prestige of the employing department and institution, are factors associated with access to resources. Gender differences in access to the resources associated with institutional location have a significant, long-term effect on publishing productivity:

> *Females have lower averages on those resources that should positively affect research productivity. Females have less selective baccalaureate institutions, less prestigious doctoral departments, less productive and prestigious mentors, and are more likely to have their career interrupted. While many of these differences are small, they are consistently in favor of males* (Long 1990, p. 1305).

Prolific scholarly writers are disproportionately likely to be employed in research institutions that offer the advantage of prestige, particularly if the faculty position is in a highly ranked department, and is equated with the availability of resources, including external sources, to support research.

The association between institutional location and resources do not operate equally for all faculty in that location (Fox 1995). Members of marginalized groups are likely to have different experiences than majority faculty in the same environment (Fox 1991; Long and Fox 1995). Even when they exist, the cross-sex nature of most mentoring relationships for women is one example of how women's experiences may be qualitatively different than those of men, even in the same academic unit or department (Clark and Corcoran 1986).

The association between institutional location, resources, and publication productivity also varies by academic field. The advantages associated with institutional location may be most pronounced in academic fields, such as the "hard" sciences, where research is affected by the quality and availability of physical resources, trained personnel, and collegial support (Wanner, Lewis, and Gregorio 1981). Although there are still advantages associated with institutional prestige, resources play a less pronounced role in academic fields where fewer resources are required to conduct research and where research tends to be a solitary activity, rather than one conducted by teams (Creamer 1997).

Environmental Factors

Recognition

As discussed in Chapter 2, national and international recognition or visibility is one element of the academic reward structure. It is central to sustaining productivity and an element that has particular influence, as will be discussed later in this section, to prolific scholarly writers. Environmental or structural factors that explain gender differences in publishing productivity are summarized in Table 4.3.

Recognition is manifested in academic rank, citations, awards, and appointments to prestigious panels and boards, fellowships, and honorary degrees (Fox 1985). The most prestigious forms of recognition come from colleagues who serve as gatekeepers or referees (Fox 1985). Membership on the editorial boards of prestigious journals or other scholarly publishing venues is also regarded as an indicator of collegial recognition (Fox 1985). As mentioned previously, only a small proportion of editors and editorial board members are women (Nicoloff and Forrest 1988; White 1984, 1985).

Differences in recognition provide one explanation for gender differences in publishing productivity (Astin 1991).

TABLE 4.3

Conceptual Explanations for Gender Differences in the Environmental Factors Associated With Publishing Productivity

Category	Explanation (Source(s))
Recognition	"Women get less payoff for publishing" in terms of recognition and visibility (Grant and Ward 1991, p. 218). Men's work is more likely to be recognized as being of scientific significance (Fox 1991).
	Women generally receive less recognition or credit than do men for their contribution to a co-authored piece, particularly with a senior male (Sonnert and Holton 1995b; Ward and Grant 1996).
Reinforcement	Lack of access of to male-controlled collegial networks limits the publication productivity of members of marginalized groups (Creswell 1985; Menges and Exum 1983).
	There are gender differences in the size of the networks, the influence or status of the networks, and the extent of the engagement with them (Cole and Zuckerman 1984).
Cumulative Advantage	The processes of initial and cumulative disadvantages may be particularly important to understanding sex and race differences in productivity (Long and Fox 1995).
	A series of small disadvantages early in the career have a long-term, cumulative impact on women's productivity (Long 1990).

The productivity gap between men and women widens because women are less recognized, particularly in the form of citations, for their work (Ward and Grant 1996).

In addition to the relationship between a sense of authority or voice, feminists have raised a closely related issue of who is acknowledged to have an authoritative voice and the role that plays in formal and informal recognition. Cognitive or scientific authority refers to who is recognized as being an expert in a field and accepted as a reliable source of information or advice. Men are more likely than women to be awarded cognitive or scientific authority (Fox 1991). Women are more likely than men to receive challenges to their authority, because they are more likely to occupy marginal positions and to be engaged in nonmainstream research (Kirsch 1993). Being perceived as an authority is a central element of recognition or visibility and an example of an element in publishing productivity that is neither individual or organizational but environmental or structural. It may help to explain why it generally takes a greater number of publications and a longer period of time for women to be recognized as senior scholars.

Reinforcement

Reinforcement or feedback, particularly from colleagues, is a critical element of the process that both initiates and sustains publishing productivity. It can be manifested through formal exchanges, such as the written comments of editors reviewing a manuscript—or it can be manifested informally, such as feedback over lunch from a colleague about an idea, or in an electronic exchange of a publication draft. Feedback from colleagues reiterates the importance of devoting time to research and writing, as well as providing an expedient way to test an idea long before the laborious process required to get the idea in print.

Although the act of writing is a solitary activity for most people, maintaining a research and publication agenda is a highly social process (Brodky 1987; Fox 1991). Collegial exchange is not just a social aspect of work performance but a critical element of it, and exclusion from such networks "limits the possibility, not simply to be part of a social circle, but rather to do research, to publish, to be cited—to show the crucial marks of productivity in science" (Fox 1991, p. 190). While colleagues internal to the institution, e final judgments about tenure and promotion, colleagues external to the institution, ultimately have the greatest role in determining national visibility and recognition.

Collaboration through co-authorship is one important source of reinforcement. Women are less likely than men to write sole authored paper and are more likely than men to co-author papers (Grant and Ward 1991). Collaboration increases dramatically with career age and as faculty become engaged in more complex, time-consuming problems and dedicate more time to mentoring graduate students and junior faculty (Bayer and Smart 1991). It varies dramatically by academic field, the nature of research problems, and the methods utilized. It is least common in academic areas, such as historical and literary scholarship, where the discourse is highly personal or dependent on personal interpretation. This compares to academic fields, such as physics or chemistry where a research question is fragmentable into small parts that can be solved by a number of people (Becher 1989). Increased levels of collaboration are found among academics pursuing scholarship that lie outside traditional, mainstream methods or topics (Becher 1989). This is one explanation of why reinforcement provided by collaboration may be particularly instrumental to the productivity of women and members of marginalized groups.

Senior faculty, who place a high priority on a research and publishing agenda, generally are actively engaged in one or more academic communities whose members center their professional and probably personal lives around reading, writing, conducting research, and publishing academic prose (Brodky 1987). They collaborate in writing articles, share drafts of manuscripts, communicate frequently, and attend similar professional meetings. Such networks have an outer circle that may number in the hundreds, while the inner circle of such networks are much smaller, consisting of six to 12 people with closely allied interests who interact frequently (Becher 1989). They exchange information about advances in knowledge, often through privately-circulated, preprints of manuscripts, long before they find their way to the public view through published articles or books.

There are gender differences, however, in the size of the networks, the influence or status of the networks, and the extent of the engagement with them (Cole and Zuckerman 1984). Both women and men pursuing nonmainstream research are likely to find reinforcement and feedback from engagement in collegial networks, but they are not as likely to be engaged in networks that involve the most influential members of the profession.

Engagement in intellectual networks or academic communities, particularly those external to the employing institution, requires resources. Among the examples of resources are supportive computer equipment to facilitate electronic exchanges, and to travel to conferences to interact with colleagues, present papers, and to keep abreast of cutting-edge developments in a field. While large-scale, external funding for support is available for scientists in some fields, it is not as readily available in the humanities and social sciences, for example, where women faculty are concentrated. Reinforcement contributes little to sustaining long-term publishing productivity without resources (Fox 1983). Pointing to the inter-relationship between reinforcement and resources:

> *Positive reinforcement can exist without cumulative advantage; but reinforcement will not account for much productivity unless accompanied by the cumulation of resources for research* (Fox 1983, p. 297).

Cumulative Advantage

The cumulative advantage perspective provides a conceptual framework to examine how characteristics of the environment, such as resources and feedback, interact to offer initial and continuing advantages associated with career advancement (Fox 1985). Although sharing many fundamental constructs with the categories that are distinguished as reinforcement and resources, the cumulative advantage perspective differs in that it focuses on the interaction of the factors. Cumulative advantage is *how* faculty are able to initiate and sustain research productivity, while reinforcement is *why* they continue to produce (Fox 1983). Reinforcement motivates continued research productivity when supported by resources that accumulate from recognition (Fox 1983).

There are two aspects of the cumulative advantage: initial advantages and cumulative advantages. Initial advantages are associated with an early start in a faculty and publishing career. These include enrollment in a prestigious doctoral program, mentoring by an eminent scholar, and early publishing success. The emphasis awarded to the role of an early start to long-term, scholarly productivity relates to the role in the processes of social stratification. Initial advantages are so critical because ". . . a scientist's standing in the stratification system is fairly well set by the end of the first decade of work" (Cole and Zuckerman 1984). The pivotal role of an early start in this stratification system is one reason that career interruptions have had such long-term, negative consequences for women's publishing productivity.

The evidence of cumulative advantages is in the widening gap between high- and low-producing academics that develops over time, as early publishing success translates to recognition and a faculty appointment in a prestigious institution, participation in prestigious collegial networks, and access to resources. Emphasizing similar, small gender differences that accumulate over time, a long-term effect on cumulative publication productivity is apparent, thereby explaining the productivity gap through a theory of "limited differences," which illustrate the series of disadvantages known as negative "kicks." It is postulated that women are more likely than men to receive negative "kicks," or career setbacks, and that women respond more negatively to these "kicks" (Cole and Singer 1991).

Cumulative advantage is the process that contributes to the formation of an elite group of academics that has in the past been highly homogenous. . . . "patterns of social selection resource, and reward help to create and maintain a class structure by providing a stratified distribution of chances for performance in science" (Fox 1975, p. 273).

The processes of initial and cumulative advantage appear to operate differently for men and women and for majority and minority faculty. For example, Schiele (1992) found that the prestige of the doctoral program was not a significant predictor of the career publishing productivity of African American social work faculty. Clark and Corcoran (1986) described tenured faculty women as "survivors" of initial disadvantage. Similarly, Long (1990) proposed that gender differences in productivity may be explained in part by a series of small disadvantages that occur early in the career. Examples are that women on average are older than men when they earn their doctorate, and they are more likely to interrupt their career, and less likely than men to have had the advantage of mentoring by an eminent, senior scholar.

Just as advantages accumulate for one group of people, disadvantages accrue for members of other groups. Patterns of disadvantage are remarkably similar across female faculty in their study, regardless of discipline, age, class, and marital status (Aisenberg and Harrington 1988).

The cumulative advantage perspective captures a process of how success breeds success or how a few, young, well-situated superstars rise to eminence. Although largely men, a few women are in this group as well, especially women affiliated with a prestigious, male mentor. The perspective offers little, though, to explain what happens to young superstars who fail to meet early promise or to explain how scholars without the advantage of early recognition, influential mentors, or institutional prestige still manage to become highly productive as academic publishers.

Summary

The impact of institutional and environmental factors on long-term publishing productivity cannot be overstated. A high level of publication output is associated with a combination of individual, institutional, and environmental or structural factors:

> *We have seen that achievement through publication is not a simple function of motivation and ability. It is the result also of organizational background, environment, and access to the means of performance—training, resources, and support* (Fox 1985, p. 273).

In this chapter, it is proposed that gender, and probably race or ethnicity, influence publishing productivity indirectly through four key institutional and environmental factors: reward, recognition, reinforcement, and resources. These factors are highly interactive. They operate differently at the outset when a record of publishing is first established and in sustaining a commitment to an agenda that awards high priority to research and publication over the full span of a career.

A summary of key points raised in this chapter and illustrated in this figure that have implications for practice are:

1. No single factor can be isolated to explain the gender gap in publication productivity that emerges when cumulative career productivity is examined. It is the accumulation of many, small disadvantages over time that uniformly favor men that explain gender differences in career publication productivity.
2. *Resources.* Of all the factors, resources is the factor that is instrumental to publishing productivity at all career phases. Resources are manifested in the opportunity to publish early in an academic career, often before entering a faculty position. Resources are also instrumental in developing and sustaining the collegial networks that are a primary vehicle for recognition and reinforcement that are central to sustaining faculty publishing produc-

... resources is the factor that is instrumental to publishing productivity at all career phases.

tivity. External resources are particularly instrumental to the productivity of faculty in disciplines where research is costly to conduct.

3. *Resources.* Rather than differences in individual qualities—for example, an interest in research—one of the primary reasons for the gender gap in publication productivity is that women are much less likely than men to be in a position with a work assignment that affords the opportunity to accomplish scholarship. This is an aspect of resources because, like training in a prestigious department where there is access to publishing opportunities with a prestigious mentor, it reflects opportunity, which was called "the means of performance" (Fox 1985, p. 273).

4. *Reinforcement and recognition.* Social and intellectual isolation inhibits publishing productivity. A faculty member may be able to initiate a publishing career without the benefit of colleagues who share her or his research interests, but they are unlikely to be able to sustain it. The effect of isolation is particularly aggravated for faculty members who are already marginalized for reasons such as their ethnicity, sexual orientation, or gender.

5. *Institutional rewards.* Institutional rewards (tenure, salary, promotion, and the consistency of their connection to publishing performance), are particularly instrumental early in a faculty member's career. Institutions are challenged to design institutional rewards that reinforce faculty for communicating the products of their scholarship throughout their careers.

6. *Recognition.* The struggle to develop assurance about having an authoritative voice and develop recognition among colleagues is often intensified by location in lower prestige departments, nontraditional appointments, and the choice of topics and methods that do not fit within dominant intellectual traditions.

Implications for Practice

The conceptual explanations for gender differences in publication productivity offer several major implications for academics called to assist new faculty members to establish a publication record, or to judge the publishing credentials of their colleagues.

1. Appointment to a temporary or adjunct faculty position are likely to have a long-term, negative impact on career publishing productivity.
2. If publishing productivity is a high priority, expectations for teaching, service, and outreach must be shaped to make it possible for a faculty member to consistently devote time to research and writing.
3. The amount of resources required to conduct research varies dramatically by academic field. Without resources, it is unrealistic to expect faculty to sustain a publication record or to develop the external, collegial network essential to national visibility and recognition.
4. Opportunities for feedback about ideas and reinforcement for the importance of publishing can be crafted by the assignment of office space, and the creation of joint space, such as conference rooms, to facilitate collegial exchange.
5. Instead of assuming that a faculty member has escaped socialization to the academic reward structure, academics such as department chairs, should anticipate skepticism about the politics involved in publishing. Also, they should acknowledge that some faculty are reluctant to utilize conventional practices that award authority; examples include self-citing or listing themselves as senior author in works co-authored with students.

Prolific authors routinely have been defined as those who have produced enough journal articles to be in the top 3 to 5 percent of all faculty in their field. Highly productive faculty might be defined as those whose number of journal articles put them in the top 25 percent of their field. At universities, about seven times more faculty men than faculty women are in the top publishing category for journal articles (see Table 1.3), and about three times more men than women faculty are in the top publishing category for book-length manuscripts (Astin, Korn, and Day 1991). The number of faculty in the top publishing category is smaller in low-consensus fields where criteria for merit are not clearly defined (Becher 1989).

The small group of prolific authors account for a relatively large proportion of articles produced in an academic field. The names of members in this group are very likely to appear on the lists of scientific honors and awards recipients in that academic field (Fox 1995). Through their presence on editorial review boards, and among the juries who review grant proposals, they have a significant influence on what is and is not published, as well as what research is awarded funding. This is the small group of people who have had a sustained presence in the literature and who have played a major role in shaping the dominant paradigms and formal discourse in an academic field.

The goal of this chapter is to understand how the individual, institutional, and environmental variables discussed in the previous chapter apply to understanding how prolific faculty manage to sustain exceptionally high levels of publishing productivity. Understanding what sustains this level of productivity is not the same as comprehending the behavior of a more typical faculty member at a doctoral-granting institution. One example is a faculty member who has produced one or two publications every two years, during the first 10 years of his or her faculty career, even though the level of publishing productivity declines rapidly after that. While the focus is most frequently on policies that initiate publishing productivity, the real challenge to universities is to design policies that sustain the productivity of more than a handful of highly-celebrated senior scholars.

Model

Figure 5.1 is used to highlight critical events associated with publishing productivity that have been isolated in the research literature described in the previous chapters as varying significantly by gender. These are events that have been characteristic of prolific scholarly writers. The key point illustrated by this table is the accumulation of small disadvantages in reward, recognition, resources, and reinforcement in critical events that explain gender differences in publishing productivity. While these also occur in the experiences of men, these disadvantages have been more likely to characterize the experience of female than male academics.

FIGURE 5.1

Key Events Associated With Prolific Publishing That Vary By Gender

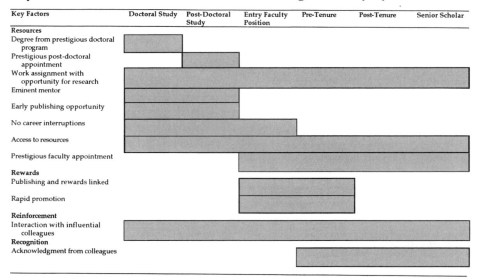

The conceptual model proposed in this figure differs in several ways from other theoretical models presented in the literature, such as the model by Blackburn and Lawrence (1996, p. 27). First, it isolates a single aspect of faculty performance—publishing productivity—rather than assuming that all aspects of faculty performance can be explained by the same set of factors. Second, it focuses on critical events, which is similar to Cole and Singer's (1991) model of limited differences. Third, it is not proposed to predict publishing productivity, but to highlight gender differences in the key events or correlates associated with publishing output. Events are only listed in the figure if there is substantial support for a history of gender differences in the research literature. This is the reason that not all correlates of faculty publishing productivity, such as individual characteristics, are shown in the figure.

Explanations for Prolific Publishing— More Like the Tortoise than the Hare

Prolific academic writers have the opportunity (called "resources" in the model presented) and the motivation to sustain a relatively high level of publishing over a long period. Although only a small subset go on to sustain that productivity, they are most likely to have initiated a successful publication record during their graduate program or earlier. These are people whose interest in research and/or publications has not been diverted to other activities for any extended period of time. They present a picture of the change in faculty productivity with age that differs from the "decay curve" illustrated in a typical histogram of the number of publications by year (Sonnertand Holton 1995, see p. 55 for an example). This is what distinguishes them from other faculty and why a separate chapter has been devoted to a discussion about them.

Sustained dedication to scholarly publishing also distinguishes the prolific writer from the highly productive academic. The academic may have established a reputation as a scholar through one or two well received publications during the first decade of their career, then shifted their talents and energies to other tasks. Rather than becoming unproductive, many of these people either divided their energies among multiple tasks, including publishing, or shifted their focus to mentoring graduate students, administrative roles, or service to the profession. This way, the prolific scholarly writer is more like the proverbial tortoise, rather than the hare in the foot race, who accumulates the quantity of publications required to achieve visibility in the profession and the status of prolific scholar.

Gender Differences Among the Prolific

While the discussion of aggregate gender differences in publishing productivity has been framed by utilizing a male-female dichotomy, it is less functional to understand the distinguishing characteristics of the group outside the mainstream who are called prolific writers. Although the main point in this text is to identify the reasons why women are missing from the ranks of the prolific, the few women who have achieved the status of being prolific probably have not done so by a route that alters dramatically from that utilized by men. It generally takes longer and requires greater output for women than men to achieve the status of being prolific. The hypothesis being presented is that the biggest gender difference *among prolific writers* is in the timing of the critical events associated with exceptional publication output, not the events themselves.

It is not uncommon in research literature about faculty publishing productivity to find authors who utilize male-only samples, but generalize the findings to all faculty. It can be argued that the critical events identified in the figure in this chapter derive from the experiences of prolific male scholars. A number of the traditional correlates, such as age and translating early recognition to long-term publishing productivity, have a much weaker predictive power for women than for men. There is little support in the existing research literature for the idea that men and women have pursued distinct paths to achieving publishing eminence.

How Faculty Sustain Publishing Productivity

From an extensive, cross-disciplinary review of the literature and concomitant research, the following is a list of characteristics of prolific scholarly authors that distinguish them from other faculty. Most of these are only summarized, because they have been reviewed in greater depth in preceding chapters. Other factors, such as external funding, are not included in the list as a separate item because they play a very prominent role in publishing productivity in some academic areas, such as the natural and physical sciences, but are not as decisive in all academic areas.

Individual characteristic—lifestyle. John Trimbur's Foreword to Gesa Kirsch's book, *Writing the Academy* (1993), suggested that, "To learn to write—in particular to learn how to write and publish and survive in the academy— is a matter not just of learning to obey a rule but also of learning a form of life" (p. ix). In the book, *Academic Writing as a Social Process,* Linda Brodkey characterized how writing and publishing can be the central organizing principle for a lifestyle when she observed members of the academic community are a specific group within the academy

". . . whose members organize their professional lives around reading, writing, and publishing academic prose."

Being a prolific writer requires sustaining a lifestyle with work as its central organizing principle. Prolific writers generally are not people who lead what others would consider a life with an equal balance between the private and public domains. What is left unsaid about that lifestyle is that it probably often sits squarely on the foundation of the labor of a spouse or partner who makes this kind of round-the-clock preoccupation possible with work by handling household responsibilities and offering untold hours of invisible labor. The senior scholar who stands at a podium in a large auditorium to be honored by a professional award and who asks his wife to rise, so that he might acknowledge that his work would not have been possible without her, is not just being gracious. He is being honest.

The support for this claim comes from the literature about the productivity of faculty men who have comparably educated wives. Being married to a comparably educated woman significantly lowers men's publishing productivity (Ferber and Huber 1979). The husband's level of education had no significant impact on women's publishing output. They reasoned that comparably educated women were more likely than those with less education to devote time to their own careers, shifting some responsibilities traditionally assumed by women to men. Similarly, Astin and Milem (1997) observed that while faculty women with an academic spouse were more productive than those with a nonacademic spouse, academic men with an academic spouse were less productive than those with a nonacademic spouse. They interpreted these findings to mean that men with nonacademic spouses have benefited from reduced household responsibilities and clerical and research support.

Possibly, with competing demands, including family responsibilities, few people are willing or able to sustain the kind of single-minded lifestyle required to be prolific over the full span of a career. One of the reasons that there are so few women among the prolific is because the expectation for this kind of lifestyle commitment is one that is hardly consistent with women's traditional roles in the family.

Individual and environmental characteristic—authority. Having something important to say, or a sense of authority in voice, is one characteristic of prolific publishers that is

Being married to a comparably educated woman significantly lowers men's publishing productivity.

developed over time and through recognition, reward, and reinforcement. Differences in the processes of recognition, reward, and reinforcement are central to understanding confirmation of intellectual authority. External validation, through the recognition awarded by senior rank, appears to be essential for women to be taken seriously by colleagues (Simeone 1987).

Institutional reward structures. In addition to socialization during graduate school and postdoctoral preparation, the institutional reward structure is most instrumental in establishing the expectation for research and publishing during the early years of a faculty member's career. The influence of institutional rewards on publishing productivity diminishes over the course of the careers of the small group of scholars who are prolific.

Resources. Most prolific faculty carry relatively light teaching loads and work largely in graduate programs. They generally have access to the labor of graduate students and/or research associates who contribute a stream of opportunities for publications. Many prolific scholars gain access to institutional resources through mobility made possible from recognition that accrues from publishing.

Environmental factors—recognition. The primary source of recognition for prolific scholars is from a community of scholars outside the home institution. Academics with the widest reputation are those whose work is known across disciplinary boundaries.

Prolific scholarly writers are the beneficiaries of a great deal of visibility and recognition for their work, generally from early in their career. Even adjusting for their high levels of output, prolific scholarly writers receive a disproportionate share of the recognition in an academic field. How benefits disproportionately accrue to those already advantaged is a phenomenon described by the label of the "Matthew Effect" (Clark and Corcoran 1986) and is a prime example of the operation of cumulative advantage.

The possibility that prolific women writers may even receive more reward and recognition than their comparable male colleagues is raised by the event history analysis of a sample of biochemists (Long, Allison, and McGinnis 1993). They concluded that "exceptionally productive women have exceptionally high probabilities of promotion, while the majority of women are less likely than comparable men to be promoted to full professor" (p. 719). This is a topic that needs further exploration, however.

Environmental factors—reinforcement. Particularly for those who are prolific, sustaining a high level of productivity is a highly social, rather than solitary, process. The productivity level of high performers is less influenced than low performers by the expectations and productivity level of departmental colleagues (Braxton 1983).

Frequent informal and formal interactions, particularly a community of scholars outside the home institution, who actively are engaged in research and scholarship, is a characteristic of most prolific scholars. In most, but not all academic areas, these communities of scholars are bound by an interest and commitment to scholarly research and writing, as much as to a highly specialized topic.

Cumulative advantage. High levels of publication productivity are the product of a combination of individual, institutional, or environmental or structural variables over time. While the cumulative advantage model focuses on the advantages associated with an early start on a faculty, research, and publishing career, issues of how this is sustained over decades have the most relevance for understanding the characteristics of prolific faculty.

Summary

Two major points are proposed in this chapter. First, the factors that initiate and sustain faculty publishing productivity are two, distinct issues. The factors primarily distinguishing prolific faculty from their colleagues is as much what they accomplish in the first 10 years of their careers, compared to their accomplishments in the last 20 years. The second key point is that both men and women, prolific publishers probably share some key characteristics and career patterns that distinguish them from their colleagues with a less singular focus, rather than distinguish them from each other. Both points need confirmation through further exploration and testing.

Implications for Practice

There are several implications for practice that emerge from the discussion presented in this chapter. First, distinct institutional policies are needed to support faculty, both to initiate and to sustain publishing productivity. Academic administrators probably have a much clearer idea about how to support the productivity of a highly acclaimed, young superstar, instead of how to sustain the productivity of the majority of faculty over the full course of a career. The factors associated with head start on a faculty career are more readily identifiable than those that sustain it.

An extension of the discussion presented in this chapter is to pose the question of the cost to departments and the faculty in those departments to successfully compete for and to retain prolific faculty in exchange for the contribution they make to departmental and institutional resources and prestige. It is very likely that highly productive faculty make contributions to the life of the academic community in a more diverse array of activities than do prolific faculty. Moderately productive publishers, or those who balance publishing with service, outreach, and teaching, receive far less attention than highly visible elite publishers who are prolific. Institutions face the challenge to examine the traditional definition of faculty productivity and to develop reward structures that acknowledge faculty who maintain a balance between the aspects of a faculty role.

IMPLICATIONS FOR PRACTICE AND FUTURE RESEARCH

Despite recognition of the role of publications in promotion at a growing number of institutions, there is no lack of cynicism about the "publish or perish mentality." Stories abound on abuses of the system, such as authors who inflate their publication counts by publishing multiple, very similar articles from the same data; the senior faculty member whose name appears on all publications from a research unit, regardless of his or her level of participation in production; the scholar who inflates his or her citation rates through self citations; or a carelessly written article, by a well-known scholar, appearing in a prestigious journal after a supposedly rigorous, author-blind, peer review. A prolific scholar, reported to have produced a book a week, for five years (Shea 1997) stretches traditional definitions about what constitutes originality and authorship, as well as an increasing number of articles with 50 to 100 co-authors (McDonald 1995). Cynicism about the politics involved in publishing may explain why faculty often express such relief about the freedom awarded by tenure to publish on topics of personal interest. It may also help to explain the so-called productivity puzzle referred to by Cole and Singer (1991) of why average faculty publishing levels are relatively low.

High levels of publication output are associated with a combination of individual, institutional, and environmental or structural factors.

The standard of being a prolific scholarly writer, or being among the top producers of journal articles in a field, is much more than a straightforward, universalistic, objective measure of merit that can be applied uniformly across academic fields. High levels of publication output are associated with a combination of individual, institutional, and environmental or structural factors. As developed through a conceptual model presented in Chapter 4, long-term gender differences in publishing productivity are associated with differences in four major correlates of productivity which vary by gender: resources, reward, recognition, and reinforcement.

Deconstructing the Language of Faculty Productivity

While it is easy to point critically to ways prolific scholars inflate their publication counts, it can be argued that they set the standard by which other faculty are judged. Traditional measures of faculty productivity rely on quantity of journal articles, reflecting the model of the natural and physical sciences where journal articles are often short, acceptance rates very high, and space in journals expanding. The mentality of counting journal articles as a primary index of faculty productivity is reinforced by practices which utilize the same measures to determine institutional rankings or prestige, such as developed by Graham and Diamond (1997).

Commonly used expressions obscure basic assumptions that are made about faculty productivity. For example, referring to scholarly productivity, when what is actually meant is a level of publishing productivity, either reveals all dimensions of faculty performance, or it is the only dimension of faculty performance that is important. A second example is the use of the term publications and journal articles interchangeably in the research literature when, in fact, what is almost always being measured is the number of journal articles published in certain, limited outlets. This obscures the reality that what counts in most academic areas is not books or book chapters but journal articles.

This discursive slight of hand could contribute to the perception that faculty's productivity decays with career age, evoking an image of deteriorating mental capacity that belies how the faculty role, particularly in terms of collaborating with students and with colleagues, changes with advancing career age. This image is a reflection of using publication productivity, particularly senior or sole-authored publications, as an exclusive measure of faculty achievement. The image of faculty work performance could be improved with external constituencies who have little knowledge about the effort and time it takes to produce a single journal article. By reconsidering the definition and the way we measure faculty productivity, a broader range of activities is acknowledged.

The conflating of all aspects of faculty performance with the term faculty productivity also contributes to the not infrequent negative reference to women faculty as being less productive than men faculty. In fact, what is meant is that, on a singe aspect of faculty performance, the discrepancy between women's and men's in comparable positions is small. However, at an aggregate level, women are significantly less likely than men to be among those who are considered to be prolific in their field and significantly more likely to be among the nonpublishers. This same type of reasoning is reflected when the lack of success of minorities in faculty positions is attributed solely to lack of scholarly productivity (Wilson 1987, cited by Patitu and Tack 1991). This is an example of the "use of paradigms, concepts, models, and methods which distort women's experiences" defined by Ward and Grant (1985, p. 141) in an article about the feminist critique of traditional research measures.

Reflecting a Male Model

During the last 20 years, a number of authors, writing about faculty productivity, have concluded that the reason prolific academic writers are almost exclusively white and male is because the measures used to define productivity reflect career paths, work assignments, interests, and access to resources that are much more characteristic of white men than women and most minorities. For example, Bayer and Astin (1975) noted, ". . . the present reward system, with its stress on the accrual of large numbers of publications and attendant phenomena, is more consistent with the professional roles and opportunities of male faculty members than of females" (p. 801). Finkelstein made a similar observation: "It would seem fair to conclude, then, that current academic compensation practices tend to recognize male strengths and female weaknesses, i.e., they are defined in terms of male strengths" (1984, p. 228).

In a review of Zuckerman, Cole, and Bruer's 1991 book, *The Outer Circle: Women in the Scientific Community,* Barbara Reskin questioned the attention in the literature to gender differences in performance:

> It seems to me that this attention to performance represents a retreat from a genuine critique of science. Attention to performance disparities usually leads to discovering how women, on average, fail to conform to that neutral ideal scientist (whose life and work patterns, of course, are modeled on male scientists). At the same time, individual level analyses blind us to how science as an institution is permeated with gendered assumptions, organized around men's life cycles, and an important source of male power in defining knowledge and legitimating the status quo (1992, p. 573).

Evelyn Fox Keller observed that culturally defined stereotypes about gender are implicit in the definition of science as impersonal, objective, and universal.

Evelyn Fox Keller observed that culturally defined stereotypes about gender are implicit in the definition of science as impersonal, objective, and universal. She noted that *"the* dilemma that has entrapped white women scientists throughout their entire history, much as it now entraps scientists (men and women) of color" is the assumption of a single, monolithic criteria for scientific performance based on publication counts (1991, p. 234).

Implications for Practice

Overt discrimination has certainly been posed as one explanation for gender and race differences in the advancement of faculty (e.g., Finkelstein 1984). Although evidence was provided in the previous chapters that institutional reward structures do not operate free of considerations of race and gender, as proposed by the universalistic norm of science, it is very likely that unequal outcomes persist, despite the efforts of individuals trying to accomplish quite the contrary. "In our view, slow progress is less the result of deliberately prejudiced actions than the failure of persons of good will to ensure equity" (Menges and Exum 1983, p. 139).

Even an entirely equitable application of traditional measures of faculty productivity to faculty hiring and promotion decisions would result in a faculty, particularly at doctoral granting institutions, that is homogenous. Gender and race differences in the impact of traditional measures of performance may be small, but the long-term, cumulative effect is substantial. These criteria do not just impact on the hiring and promotion of an occasional woman or minority, but that they systematically impact members of certain groups.

Recommendations to expand traditional criteria used to evaluate publication productivity in faculty hiring and promotion decisions appear in the next chapter. The resistance to revising traditional hiring and promotion criteria is substantial, not only because they are valued as objective measures but also because the existing pool of candidates is so great that it is relatively easy in many fields to find applicants who meet, if not exceed, traditional criteria. The following sections provide examples of traditional hiring and promotion criteria that are likely to have the unanticipated outcome of systematically restricting the number of women and minorities who are deemed to be competitive.

Criteria that Systematically Eliminate Women and Minorities in a Hiring Pool

The following criteria routinely applied in faculty hiring decisions are much more likely to result in the selection of a man than a woman:

1. Look for a candidate who is on the "fast track." Expect the candidate to have earned a doctorate within 10 years of completing a baccalaureate degree, or by the time he or she is 30 years old.
2. Use scholarly publications—in graduate school or before—as a key indicator of potential and ability to publish.
3. Expect that one of the letters of recommendation is from a mentor who is an eminent scholar in the field.
4. Disqualify anyone whose doctorate was not earned from a prestigious institution or department.
5. View career interruptions, including periods of unemployment, as a sign that the candidate has not clearly defined his or her career goals.

Criteria that Systematically Block the Promotion of Women and Minorities

Similarly, many traditional criteria used to evaluate faculty for promotion are also much more characteristic of men than women. The following criteria are much more likely to support the promotion of men than women:

1. Utilize the number of citations to the candidate's work as a major criterion for evaluation.
2. Assume that the candidate only took a major conceptual role in articles where he or she appears as the senior or sole author. Devalue collaboration with students.
3. Expect the topic of scholarly research to be embedded in an area with a lengthy intellectual tradition.
4. Regardless of academic field, rely on total journal article production as a primary measure of productivity. Ignore other types of scholarly communication because they cannot be verified by readily available sources.
5. Expect letters from external referees to be from eminent, male scholars in the field.
6. Expect all faculty, regardless of topic or research method utilized, to be well established as a scholarly publisher within five years of their first faculty appointment.
7. Disregard teaching load and service responsibilities when establishing whether the candidate meets the minimum level of publishing productivity required for promotion.

Expanding the Definition of Scholarship

Diversifying the faculty requires diversifying the criteria used to judge their performance. Although it is not within the scope of this monograph to explore other aspects of faculty performance, such as teaching and service, or how they might be balanced in the reward system, there are, nevertheless, a number of ways academics can shape institutional policies in ways that expand what it means to make a contribution to knowledge and to recognize multiple ways that research and scholarship is communicated. Modifications to traditional definitions of faculty publishing productivity are likely to recognize the contributions of a more diverse group of men, as well as women faculty.

Scholarship Reconsidered (Boyer, 1990) and *Scholarship Assessed* (Glassick, Huber, and Maeroff 1997) are two publications from the Carnegie Foundation for the Advancement of Teaching that were part of the call to expand the definition of what is rewarded as scholarship. Boyer (1990) proposed four separate, overlapping, categories of scholarship: (a) the scholarship of discovery, (b) the scholarship of integration, (c) the scholarship of application, and (d) the scholarship of teaching. The first category has been traditionally defined as the most prestigious form of scholarship, which is contributing to the body of new knowledge through the communication of findings from original research. The second, the scholarship of integration, is illustrated by monographs, which strive to synthesize knowledge across disciplinary boundaries and to interpret scholarship for an audience of nonspecialists. The third, the scholarship of application, recognizes faculty responsibility for outreach and suggests recognition of knowledge that improves practice. The fourth encourages scholarship about teaching and pedagogy.

Definition of Usefulness

As discussed in Chapter 3, impact or usefulness of a faculty member's work is one of the primary measures used to judge faculty research performance. However, usefulness almost exclusively has been judged by the extent that the work is cited by other scholars in the field.

Consistent with Boyer's (1990) proposal, an expanded definition of usefulness would recognize academics as just one of several communities that are impacted by the production of knowledge. Peer evaluations could be extended to include members of these wider audiences. Other communities include practitioners or nonacademics in the field, as well as referencing patterns in unpublished work produced by graduate students or shared in presentations at conferences. In some fields, impact could be assessed by the extent an author's work is referenced in proceedings of related national or international conferences or through services, such as the ERIC Clearinghouse, that abstract such presentations.

Definition of Recognized Modes of Scholarly Communication

When when weighed by the prestige of the journal, output of articles in refereed journals is awarded the highest priority to formal communication among scholars in similar fields or specialties. Relying on citations as a measure of quality or impact further limits the collegial exchange that is officially rewarded or recognized. In many fields, particularly those where knowledge changes rapidly, other forms of scholarly communication, such as the exchange of manuscript drafts, or preprints of articles, define the cutting edge of knowledge. Electronic journals and exchanges are moving in the forefront of academic discourse in some fields. Public presentations at conferences or through invited speeches are also examples of scholarly exchange that advance knowledge.

Acknowledgment of Diverse Career Paths

The traditional model of a faculty career path that identifies the potential super star begins with the initial advantages of enrollment in a prestigious doctoral program, mentoring by an eminent, senior male scholar in the field, and an early start on a faculty and publishing career. Early recognition through publishing success translates to an appointment in a prestigious department, invitations to become involved in influential networks, and access to internal and external institutional resources. This is a career path that is much less likely to characterize the experiences of women who are, on average, older when they earn a doctorate, more likely to interrupt their career, less likely to graduate from a prestigious doctoral program and mentored by a senior scholar, but more likely to be employed in nontenure track positions than men (Long 1990).

The failure to recognize diverse career paths, and the assumption that career paths defined as nontraditional indi-

The failure to recognize diverse career paths, and the assumption that career paths defined as nontraditional indicate a lack of focus or motivation, is a clear example of how patterns are most typical of men.

cate a lack of focus or motivation, is a clear example of how patterns are most typical of men. These patterns are largely developed in the physical and natural sciences, and they are applied as a norm across many academic areas.

Development of Distinct Performance Standards By Academic Field

As discussed throughout this text, there are substantial disciplinary differences in the way knowledge is generated and communicated. Among the examples are the amount of resources required to conduct research, collaboration patterns, type of publication that is the primary mode of communicating knowledge, typical length of publications, and acceptance rates in the most prestigious journals. Comparisons of journal article productivity rates across academic areas tends to exaggerate gender and race differences in publishing productivity. This involves ignoring the effect of the concentration of women and minorities at lower ranks, and in academic areas and institutions where journal article production is not rewarded.

Examples of Diverse Criteria

The following performance criteria value the credentials of a diverse faculty:

1. Look for evidence of the breadth of dissemination of ideas, including to academic audiences but also to nonacademics, such as practitioners in the field.
2. Ask the candidates to select a few publications that they consider to be exemplary and evaluate the publications by peers, instead of using quantity of publications as the main index research performance.
3. Include a broad range of measures that indicate participation in scholarly exchange. Examples are journal articles, books, and unpublished documents, such as pre-prints, electronic exchanges, and abstracts from conference presentations.
4. In addition to publications and activities that contribute to new knowledge, acknowledge the contribution of the three other types of scholarship identified by Boyer (1990).
5. Reward co-authorship as much as sole or senior authorship, recognizing the contribution to quality of multiple

backgrounds and viewpoints to original scholarship, as well as the evidence it provides of mentoring when a publication is co-authored with a student.

6. Select candidates with advanced degrees from a variety of programs.
7. Examine the dissertation, or unpublished writing produced during graduate school, for evidence of the potential and skills necessary to publish and conduct research.
8. Recognize the potential for contribution from candidates who bring diverse career paths to a position.
9. Expand peer evaluation to include members of diverse audiences.

Need for Research

With such an exploding empirical research base, it is not surprising that there are multiple gaps in the research literature about correlates of publishing productivity and how they vary by gender and race. Research on the topic of variations in publication productivity by gender and race can be expanded by (a) broadening the range of academic fields studied, (b) utilizing qualitative research methods, (c) exploring differences among cohort groups, and (d) examining correlates of a full spectrum of scholarly publications employed to communicate knowledge.

Reflecting the esteem in which scientists are held, or possibly the existence of clear indicators of extraordinary performance, or the agenda of external funding sources, much of the most substantial and widely recognized research about faculty publishing productivity has been conducted among physical scientists, particularly among chemists and biochemists. To enlarge the discussion of variations by academic field, as well as to incorporate emerging fields, it is important that research is conducted about the scholarly writing of faculty in the full range of academic areas. A broader investigation of faculty performance in what is described as low-consensus fields, or fields where there is an expansive range of theoretical and research paradigms, will offer the opportunity to more fully explore the experiences of women and minority faculty. Expanding the scope of disciplines studied is probably the only way that sample sizes can be large enough to reach any conclusions about the productivity of minority faculty.

Ease of access of information through published sources, the availability of data from national faculty surveys, and the drive to find a unit of measurement that crosses disciplines, have contributed to the emphasis on quantitative methods to explore publishing productivity, as well as focus on journal articles as the primary unit for analysis of faculty productivity. Very little qualitative research has been published about the correlates of publishing productivity, particularly to examine how these operate over the span of a career. Case studies, life histories, and biographical or autobiographical writing can provide ways to examine the broader institutional and environmental context of scholarly writing.

Much of the research about faculty publishing productivity uses a cross sectional design that aggregates faculty at varying career stages without considering variations by age or cohort group. Evidence of the narrowing of the gender gap in publications in some fields, the increase in the representation of women on the faculty in some academic fields, and the evolving attitudes about women and work, underscore the intuitive recognition that there are undoubtedly significant differences in the experiences of women faculty by cohort groups. These differences are not tapped even by ambitious, longitudinal research studies. Exploring gender and race differences in resources, reward, recognition, and reinforcement among men and women entering faculty positions at different periods of time would be a powerful way to develop rich data to test the model proposed in Chapter 4.

One way to position women more centrally in the discussion about publication productivity is to more fully examine other types of scholarly communication, particularly the production of longer, book-length manuscripts. This is likely to enhance the recognition of the scholarship produced by women, because they have a greater presence, partly because of disciplinary location, among book authors than among journal article authors. Considerably less research has been published about the correlates of types of scholarly publications other than journal articles, such as book and book-length manuscripts, and how these vary from the correlates of journal article productivity. Similarly, it is not clear how different types of publications contribute to national visibility among a wide audience and how these vary by gender and race.

A number of disturbing implications emerged from the synthesis of the research about the correlates of faculty that have particular implications for women and minority faculty. One is that partly because their numbers are so small, especially among tenure track faculty at doctoral granting institutions, the number of relatively recent, readily available publications about race and publishing productivity is astonishingly small. Anther disturbing finding about same-sex, same-race citation patterns, noted in Chapter 3, suggest the need for research about intellectual isolation and the extent that collegial networks are sex and race segregated. References listed in published and unpublished documents could be used to test the hypotheses that the majority of women's scholarship reaches audiences that are primarily female, and that the scholarship of minority faculty is largely utilized by other minority faculty.

It is easy to be suspicious that traditional measures of faculty productivity, especially in fields where the acceptance rate of articles by refereed journals hover at the intensely competitive level of 10 percent or less, do as much to discourage as to reward faculty motivation to publish. Research about the change in faculty publication patterns before and after earning tenure, particularly to the extent they are considered mainstream, and variations by gender and race offer one way to test this hypothesis.

Conclusion

The issue of universalism and particularism appears throughout the literature in the sociology of science about gender and race differences in faculty productivity. Universalism is a norm of science that suggests that faculty rewards for knowledge production are based on scientific merit, rather than particularistic criteria such a gender or race (Braxton 1993). Personal attributes, such as gender and race, are most likely to influence hiring and promotion decisions in academic fields where there are no clear performance criteria, or consensus about what constitutes good scholarship.

It is the context of the discussion about particularism and universalism that the question is raised as to whether the low participation and recognition of women and minorities in science can be explained by the failure to demonstrate scientific merit or the application of particularistic, rather than universal, criteria of performance. Long and Fox (1995) posed the key question as, "To what extent is the inequality in science equitable or inequitable?" (p. 46). In addition to looking at the question of whether the criteria are applied equitably, it is necessary to raise the question of whether the criteria themselves are actually universal. This challenges the criteria that are used and whether they are applied discriminately or equally.

A second major issue raised about faculty productivity is whether the primary faculty roles of teaching, service, and research are mutually compatible or competitive for most faculty. The public's concern that faculty members are preoccupied with research is countered, not by the fact that the majority of faculty balance multiple roles, but by argument that teaching and research are inter-related, and the assertion that the good teacher is the good researcher. While the acknowledgment of institutional status and prestige are measured by the graduate function, it belies the reality that faculty most likely to be recognized as distinguished, by virtue of their publication record, are those who have a work assignment suited to it. They are largely faculty who have an appointment in a graduate program, possess a highly specialized research focus, consider research more important than teaching, and spend less time teaching and providing service than their less prolific counterparts. This, once again, raises the central question of why institutions continue to cling to a unidimensional standard of faculty performance that rewards the accumulation of highly specialized publications, directed to a small audience of colleagues, and devalue the contribution of faculty members who manage to maintain a research agenda, while simultaneously being actively engaged in service and teaching.

REFERENCES

The Educational Resources Information Center (ERIC) Clearinghouse on Higher Education abstracts and indexes the current literature on higher education for inclusion in ERIC's database and announcement in ERIC's monthly bibliographic journal, *Resources in Education* (RIE). Most of these publications are available through the ERIC Document Reproduction Service (EDRS). For publications cited in this bibliography that are available from EDRS, ordering number and price code are included. Readers who wish to order a publication should write to the ERIC Document Reproduction Service, 7420 Fullerton Road, Suite 110, Springfield, Virginia 22153-2852. (Phone orders with VISA or MasterCard are taken at 800/443-ERIC or 703/440-1400.) When ordering, please specify the document (ED) number. Documents are available as noted in microfiche (MF) and paper copy (PC). If you have the price code ready when you call, EDRS can quote an exact price. The last page of the latest issue of *Resources in Education* also has the current cost, listed by code.

Aisenberg, N. and Harrington, M. 1988. *Women of academe: Outsiders in the sacred grove.* Amherst, MA: The University of Massachusetts Press.

Aisenberg, N., and Harrington, M. Reprinted in J. S. Glazer, E.M. Bensimon, B. K. Townsend (Eds.), 1993, *Women in higher education: A feminist perspective* (pp. 387–398). Needham Heights: MA: ASHE Reader Series, Ginn Press.

Astin, A.W., Korn, W. S., Day, E. L. 1991. The American college teacher: National norms for the 1989–1990 HERI faculty survey. Los Angeles: Higher Education Research Institute. ED 351 906. 163 pp. MF–01; PC not available from ERDS.

Astin, H. S. 1969. *The woman doctorate in America.* New York: Russell Sage Foundation.

Astin, H. S. 1978. Factors affecting women's scholarly productivity. In H. S. Astin and W. Z. Hirsch (Eds.), *The higher education of women: Essays in honor of Rosemary Park* (pp.133–157). NY: Praeger Publishers.

Astin, H.S. 1984. The meaning of work in women's lives: A sociopsychological model of career choice and work behavior. *The Counseling Psychologist,* 12(4), 117–126.

Astin, H.S. 1991. Citation classics: Women's and men's perceptions of their contributions to science. In H. Zuckerman, J. R. Cole, and J .T. Bruer (Eds.), *The outer circle: Women in the scientific community* (pp. 57–70). NY: Norton.

Astin, H.S. and Davis, D. E. 1985. Research productivity across the life and career cycles: Facilitator and barriers for women.

Reprinted in J. S. Glazer, E.M. Bensimon, B. K. Townsend (Eds.), (1993), *Women in higher education: A feminist perspective* (pp. 415–423). Needham Heights, MA: ASHE Reader Series, Ginn Press.

Astin, H.S., and Milem, J. F. 1997. The status of academic couples in U.S. institutions. In M.A. Ferber and J. W. Loeb (Eds.), *Academic couples: Problems and promises* (pp. 128–155). Urbana, IL: University of Illinois Press.

Baird, L. L. 1991. Publication productivity in doctoral research departments: Interdisciplinary and intradisciplinary factors. *Research in Higher Education, 32,* 303–318.

Bayer, A. E., and Astin, H.S. (1975). Sex differentials in the academic reward system. *Science, 188,* 796–802.

Bayer, A. E., and Smart, J. C. 1991. Career publication patterns and collaborative 'styles' in American academic science. *Journal of Higher Education, 62,* 613–636.

Bean, J.P., and Kuh, G.D. 1988. The relationship between author gender and the methods and topics used in the study of college students. *Research in Higher Education, 28,* 130–144.

Becher, T. 1989. *Academic tribes and territories.* Bristol, PA: Open University Press.

Bentley, R. J., and Blackburn, R. T. 1990. Changes in academic research performance over time: A study of institutional accumulative advantage. *Research in Higher Education, 31,* 327–345.

Bentley, R. J., and Blackburn, R. T. 1992. Two decades of gains for female faculty? *Teachers College Record, 93*(4), 697–709.

Bieber, J.P., and Blackburn, R. T. 1993. Faculty research productivity 1972–1988: Development and application of constant units of measure. *Research in Higher Education, 34,* 551–567.

Biglan, A. 1973. The characteristics of subject matter in different academic areas. *Journal of Applied Psychology,* 57(3), 195–203.

Blackburn, R. T., Behymer, C. E., and Hall, D. E. 1978. Research note: Correlates of faculty publications. *Sociology of Education, 51,* 132–141.

Blackburn, R. T., Bieber, J.P., Lawrence, J. H., and Trautvetter, L. 1991. Faculty at work: Focus on research, scholarship, and service. *Research in Higher Education, 32,* 385–413.

Blackburn, R. T., and Lawrence, J. H. 1996. *Faculty at Work.* Baltimore, MD: The Johns Hopkins University Press.

Blackburn, R., Wenzel, S. and Bieber J. P. 1994. Minority vs. majority faculty publication performance: A research note. *The Review of Higher Education, 17,* 271–282.

Boyer, E. L. 1990. *Scholarship reconsidered: Priorities of the pro-*

fessoriate. Princeton, NJ: The Carnegie Foundation for the Advancement of Teaching. ED 326 149. 151 pp. MF–01; PC not available from EDRS.

Braxton, J. M. 1983. Department colleagues and individual faculty publication productivity. *The Review of Higher Education, 6*, 115–128.

Braxton, J. M. 1993. Deviancy from the norms of science: The effects of anomie and alienation in the academic profession. *Research in Higher Education, 32* (2), 213–228.

Braxton, J. M., and Bayer, A. E. 1986. Assessing faculty scholarly performance. In J. W. Creswell (Ed.), *Measuring faculty research performance* (pp. 25–42). New Directions for Institutional Research, No. 50. San Francisco: Jossey–Bass.

Braxton, J. M.,and Hargens, L. L. 1996. In J. Smart (Ed.), *Higher education: Handbook of theory and research, Vol. XI,* (pp. 1–46). Edison, NJ: Agathon.

Brodkey, L. 1987. *Academic writing as a social process.* Philadelphia, PA: Temple University Press.

Budd, J. M. 1990. Higher education literature. Characteristics of citation patterns. *Journal of Higher Education, 61,* 84–97.

Clark, S.M. and Corcoran, M. 1986. Perspectives on the professional socialization of women faculty: A case of accumulative disadvantage? Reprinted in J. S. Glazer, E.M. Bensimon, B. K. Townsend (Eds.), 1993, (pp. 399–414). Needham Heights, MA: ASHE Reader Series, Ginn Press.

Cole, J. R. 1979. *Fair science: Women in the scientific community.* New York: The Free Press.

Cole, S. 1979. Age and scientific performance. *American Journal of Sociology, 84,* 958–977.

Cole, J. R., and Cole, S. 1973. *Social stratification in science.* Chicago: University of Chicago.

Cole, J. R., and Singer, B. 1991. A theory of limited differences: Explaining the productivity puzzle in science. In H. Zuckerman, J. R. Cole, and J. T. Bruer (Eds.), *The outer circle:Women in the scientific community* (pp. 277–310). New York: Norton.

Cole, J. R. and Zuckerman, H. 1984. The productivity puzzle: persistence and change in patterns of publications of men and women scientists. *Advances in Motivation and Achievement, 2,* 217–258.

Cole, J. R., and Zuckerman, H. 1987, February. Marriage, motherhood, and research performance in science. *Scientific American,* 119–125.

Collins, P.H. 1983. Learning from the outsider within: The sociologi-

---

cal significance of black feminist thought. *Social Problems, 33*(6), 514–532.

Creamer, E.G. 1994. Gender and publications in core higher education journals. *Journal of College Student Development, 35,* 35–39.

Creamer, E.G. 1995. The scholarly productivity of female academics. *Initiatives (Journal of the National Association of Women in Education), 57*(1), 1–9.

Creamer, E.G. 1996. The perceived contribution of academic partners to women's publishing productivity. Paper presented at the 1996 annual meeting of the Association for the Study of Higher Education. Memphis, TN. ED 403 787. 26 pp. MF–01; PC–02.

Creamer, E.G., and Engstrom, C.M. 1996. Institutional factors women academics perceive to be associated with their publishing productivity. ED 405 755. 22 pp. MF–01; PC–01.

Creswell, J. W. 1985. *Faculty research performance: Lessons from the sciences and social sciences.* ASHE–ERIC Higher Education Report No. 4. Washington, DC: Association for the Study of Higher Education. ED 267 677. 92 pp. MF–01; PC–04.

Davis, D. E., and Astin, H.S. 1987. Reputational standing in academe. *Journal of Higher Education, 58,* 261–275.

Dill, D.D. 1986. Research as a scholarly activity: Context and Culture. In J. W. Creswell (Ed.), *Measuring faculty research performance* (pp. 7–24). New Directions for Institutional Research, No. 50. Volume XIII, No. 2. San Francisco: Jossey Bass Publishers.

Dupagne, M. 1993. Gender differences in predicting productivity of faculty. *Journalism Educator, 48*(1), 37–45.

Dwyer, M.M., Flynn, A. A., and Inman, P.S. 1991. Differential progress of women faculty: Status 1980–1990. In J. Smart (Ed.), *Higher education: Handbook of theory and research, Vol. 7,* (pp. 173–222). Edison, NJ: Agathon.

Elmore, C. J., and Blackburn, R. T. 1983. Black and white faculty in white research universities. *Journal of Higher Education, 54,* 1–15.

Ferber, M.A. 1986. Citations: Are they an objective measure of scholarly merit. *Signs: Journal of Women in Culture and Society, 11,* 381–389.

Ferber, M.A. 1988. Citations and networking. *Gender & Society, 2,* 82–89.

Ferber, M.A., and Loeb, J. W. 1973. Performance, rewards, and perceptions of sex discrimination among male and female faculty. *American Journal of Sociology, 78,* 995–1002.

Ferber, M.A., and Loeb, J. W. 1979. Husbands, wives, and careers.

Journal of Marriage and Family, 41 (May), 315–325.

Finkelstein, M. J. 1984. The status of academic women: An assessment of five competing explanations. *The Review of Higher Education, 7,* 224–245.

Fox, M. F. 1983. Publication productivity among scientists: A critical review. *Social Studies of Science, 13,* 285–305.

Fox, M.F. 1985. Publication, performance, and reward in science and scholarship. In J. C. Smart (Ed.), *Higher education: Handbook of theory and research, Vol 1,* (pp. 225–283). New York: Agathon Press.

Fox, M.F. 1991. Gender, environmental milieu, and productivity in science. In H. Zuckerman, J. R. Cole, and J. T. Bruer (Eds.), *The outer circle: Women in the scientific community* (pp. 188–204). NY: Norton.

Fox, M.F. 1992. Research, teaching, and publication productivity: Mutuality versus competition in academia. *Sociology of Education, 65,* 293–305.

Fox, M. F. 1995. Women and scientific careers. In S. Jasanoff, G. E. Markle, J. C. Petersen, and T. Pinch (Eds.), *Handbook of science and technology studies* (pp. 205–223). Thousand Oaks, CA: Sage Publications.

Fox, M.F., and Faver, C.A. 1985. Men, women, and publication productivity: Patterns among social work academics. *The Sociological Quarterly, 26*(4), 537–549.

Fox, M.F., and Ferri, V.C. 1992. Women, men, and their attributions for success in academe. *Social Psychology Quarterly, 55*(3), 257–271.

Garland, K. 1990. Gender differences in scholarly publication among faculty in ALA accredited library schools. *Library and Information Science Research, 12,* 155–166.

Glassick, C.E., Huber, M.T., and Maeroff, G.I. 1997. *Scholarship assessed: Evaluation of the professoriate.* An Ernest L. Boyer Project of the Carnegie Foundation for the Advancement of Teaching. San Francisco: Jossey-Bass Publishers.

Graham, H. D., and Diamond, N. 1997. *The rise of American research universities.* Baltimore, MD: Johns Hopkins University Press.

Grant, L., and Ward, K. B. 1991. Gender and publishing in sociology. *Gender & Society, 5,* 207–223.

Hamovitch, W., and Morgenstern, R. D. 1977. Children and productivity of academic women. *Journal of Higher Education, 48,* 633–645.

Hargens, L. L. 1988. Scholarly consensus and journal rejection rates.

American Sociological Review, 53, 139–151.

Hargens, L. L. 1990. Variation in journal peer review systems: Possible causes and consequences. *Journal of the American Medical Association, 263*(10), 1348–1352.

Hargens, L. L., Mc Cann, J. C., and Reskin, B.F. 1978. Productivity and reproductivity: Fertility and professional achievement among research scientists. *Social Forces, 57,* 154–163.

Helmreich, R. L., Spence, J.T., Beane, W. E., Lucher, G. W., and Matthews, K. A. 1980. Making it in academic psychology: Demographic and personality correlates of attainment. *Journal of Personality and Social Psychology, 39,* 896–908.

Hickson, M. III, Stacks, D. W., and Amsbary, J. H. 1992. Active prolific female scholars in communication: An analysis of research productivity, II. 1992. *Communication Quarterly, 40,* 350–356.

Hickson, M. III, Stacks, D. W., and Amsbary, J. H. 1993. Active prolific scholars in communication studies: Analysis of research productivity, II. *Communication Quarterly, 42,* 225–233.

Hunter, D. E. 1986. Women who write: Prolific female scholars in higher education and student affairs administration. *Journal of the National Association for Women Deans, Administrators, and Counselors, 50*(1), 33–39.

Hunter, D. E., and Kuh, G. D. 1987. The "Write wing": Characteristics of prolific contributors to the higher education literature. *Journal of Higher Education, 58,* 443–462.

Hutchinson, B.E., and Zivny, T.L. 1995. The publication profile of economists. *The Journal of Economic Education, 26*(1), 59–79.

Keller, E. F. 1991. The woman scientist: Issues of sex and gender in the pursuit of science. In H. Zuckerman, J. R. Cole, and J. T. Bauer (Eds.), *The outer circle: Women in the scientific community* (pp. 227–236). New York: Norton & Company.

Kirsch, G. E. 1993. *Women writing the academy: Audience, authority, and transformation.* Carbondale, IL: Southern Illinois University Press.

Knoppers, A. 1989. Productivity and collaborative patterns of physical educators. *Research Quarterly For Exercise and Sport, 60*(2), 159–165.

Korytnyk, C. A. 1988. Comparison of the publishing patterns between men and women Ph.D.s in librarianship. *Library Quarterly, 58*(1), 52–65.

Kyvik, S. 1990. Motherhood and scientific productivity. *Social Studies of Science, 20,* 149–160.

Liebowitz, S. J., and Palmer, J. P. 1988. Assessing assessment of economics departments. *Quarterly review of economics and business, 28,* 88–113.

Lloyd, M. E. 1990. Gender factors in reviewer recommendations for manuscript publication. *Journal of Applied Behavior Analysis, 23,* 539–543.

Long, J. S. 1990. The origins of sex differences in science. *Social Forces, 68,* 1297–1315.

Long, J. S. 1992. Measures of sex differences in scientific productivity. *Social Forces, 71,* 159–178.

Long, J. S., Allison, P.D., and McGinnis, R. 1993. Rank advancement in academic careers: Sex differences and the effects of productivity. *American Sociological Review, 58,* 703–722.

Long, J. S., and Fox, M. F. 1995. Scientific careers: universalism and particularism. *Annual Review of Sociology, 21,* 45–71.

Lutz, C. 1990. The erasure of women's writing in sociocultural anthropology. *American Ethnologist, 17,* 611–627.

Mac Kinnon, C. 1987. *Feminism Unmodified.* Cambridge, MA: Harvard University Press.

McDonald, K. A. 1995, April 28. Too many co-authors? *The Chronicle of Higher Education,* pp. A35–A36.

Menges, R. J. and Exum, W. H. 1983. Barriers to the progress of women and minority faculty. *Journal of Higher Education, 54,* 123–144.

Mooney, C.J. 1991, May 22. In two years, a million refereed articles, 300,000 books, chapters, monographs. *The Chronicle of Higher Education,* p. A17.

Nettles, M.T., and Perna, L. W. 1995. Sex and race differences in faculty salaries, tenure, rank, and productivity: Why, on average, do women, African Americans, and Hispanics have lower salaries, tenure, and rank? Paper presented at the annual meeting of the Association for the Study of Higher Education. ERIC Document: ED 391 402. 48 pp. MF–01; PC–02.

Newell, L. J., and Kuh, G. D. 1989. Taking stock: The higher education professoriate. *The Review of Higher Education, 13*(1), 63–90.

Nicoloff, L. K. and Forrest, L. 1988. Gender issues in research and publication. *Journal of College Student Personnel, 29,* 521–528.

Omundson, J. S., and Mann, G. J. 1994. Publication productivity and promotion of accounting faculty women: A comparative study. *Journal of Education for Business, 70,* 17–24.

Park, S.M. 1996. Research, teaching, and service: Why shouldn't women's work count? *Journal of Higher Education, 67,* 46–84.

Patitu, C. L., and Tack, M. W. 1991. Job satisfaction of African-American faculty in higher education in the south. Paper presented at the annual meeting for the Association for the Study of Higher Education. Boston. ERIC Document: ED 339 318. 25 pp. MF–01; PC–01.

Pearson, W., Jr. 1985. *Black scientists, white society, and colorless science.* Millwood, NY: Associated Faculty Press.

Persell, C.H. 1983. Gender, rewards and research in education. *Psychology of Women Quarterly, 8*(1), 33–47.

Radhakrishna, R. B., and Jackson, G. B. 1995. Prolific authors in the *Journal of Agricultural Education*: A review of the eighties. *Journal of Agricultural Education, 36*(1), 55–63.

Ransom, M. R. 1990. Gender segregation by field in higher education. *Research in Higher Education, 31*(5), 477–494.

Reskin, B.F. 1978. Scientific productivity, sex, and location in the institution of science. *American Journal of Sociology, 83,* 1235–1243.

Reskin, B.F. 1992. Women in science: Conflicting views on where and why. *Journal of Contemporary Sociology, 21*(5), 571–573.

Richardson, P., Parker, R. S., and Udell, G. G. 1992, November/December. Does research enhance or inhibit teaching? An exploratory study. *Journal of Education for Business,* 79–83.

Robinson, A. 1996. Perceived factors that influence achievement of tenure for African American faculty at Virginia Polytechnic Institute and Old Dominion University. *UMI Dissertation Services.* (UMI No. 9624230)

Schiele, J. H. 1991. Publication productivity of African-American social work faculty. *Journal of Social Work Education, 27*(2), 125–134.

Schiele, J. H. 1992. Scholarly productivity and social work doctorates: Patterns among African Americans. *Journal of Multicultural Social Work, 2*(4), 75–90.

Schuster, J. H., and Bowen, H.R. 1985. The faculty at risk. *Change, 17*(4), 13–21.

Shea, C. 1997, May. For these scholarly authors, more is better. *The Chronicle of Higher Education,* pp. A13–A14.

Silverman, R. J. 1987. How we know what we know: A study of higher education journals. *The Review of Higher Education, 11,* 39–59.

Simeone, A. 1987. *Academic women: Working towards equality.* South Hadley, MA: Bergin and Garvey.

Smart, J. C. 1991. Gender equity in academic rank and salary. *The Review of Higher Education, 14,* 511–526.

Smart, J. C., and Bayer, A. E. 1986. Author collaboration and impact: A note on citation rates of single and multiple authored articles. *Scientometrics, 10*(5–6), 297–305.

Smith, E. 1991. A comparative study of occupational stress from a sample of black and white U.S. college and university faculty. *Research in Race and Ethnic Relations, 6,* 145–163.

Sonnert, G. and Holton, G. 1995a. *Gender differences in science careers: The project access study.* New Brunswick, NJ: Rutgers University Press.

Sonnert, G. and Holton, G. 1995b. *Who succeeds in science?: The gender dimension.* New Brunswick, NJ: Rutgers University Press.

The Committee on the Status of Women in the Economics Profession. 1980. *American Economic Review, 70*(2), 466–474.

The Chronicle of Higher Education Almanac Issue. 1996, September 2. Vol XLIII, No 1.

Thomas, F. N., and Kenzie, P.N. 1986. Prolific writers in marital and family therapy: A research note. *Journal of Marital and Family Therapy, 12*(2), 175–180.

Toutkoushian, R. K. 1994. Using citations to measure sex discrimination in faculty salaries. *Review of Higher Education, 18,* 61–82.

Toren, N. 1991. The nexus between family and work roles of academic women in Israel: Reality and representation. *Sex Roles, 24,* 651–667.

Walters, C.G., Fry, E. H., and Chaisson, B.D. 1990. Women scholars: Closing the publication gap. *Research in Higher Education, 31,* 355–367.

Wanner, R. A., Lewis, L. S., and Gregorio, D. I. 1981. Research productivity in academia: A comparative study of the sciences, social sciences and humanities. *Sociology of Education, 54,* 238–253.

Ward, K. B., and Grant, L. 1985. The feminist critique and a decade of published research in sociological journals. *The Sociological Quarterly, 26,* 139–157.

Ward, K. B., Gast, J., and Grant, L. 1992. Visibility and dissemination of women's scholarship. *Social Problems, 39*(3), 291–298.

Ward, K. B., and Grant, L. 1996. Gender and academic publishing. In J. Smart (Ed.), *Higher education: Handbook of theory and research, Vol. XI,* (pp. 172–212). Edison, NJ: Agathon.

White, A. 1984. Where have all the women writers gone? *The Personnel and Guidance Journal, 62,* 631–636.

White, A. 1985. Women as authors and editors of psychological journals. *American Psychologist, 40*(5), 527–530.

INDEX

A

Academic Fields

Development of Distinct Performance Standards by, 78

with highest percentage faculty across institutional types, 10

Academic men with an academic spouse

less productive than those with a nonacademic spouse, 67

Academic Writing as a Social Process, 66

Accountants

criteria used to assess publishing productivity in, 6

gender differences in Mean Journal Article Productivity, 7

no significant gender differences in publishing productivity, 14

ACE. *See* American Council of Education

Acknowledgment of Diverse Career Paths, 77–78

African American faculty

promotion rates lower than promotion rates for all, 22

employment of, 17

in social work published less than all social work

doctorates but much higher percentage nonpublished, 18

mean productivity less than white in all three fields, 18

African American writers

perception that works are subjective and unscholarly, 17

age of citation, 35–36

Aisenberg and Harrington (1988)

women as being the "informed outsider," 51

American Council of Education, 7

survey of faculty, 9

Anthropology

females producing one-fourth of the publications but only

received about one-fifth of the citations, 38–39

one of least male dominated disciplines, 40

only one classic was authored by a woman in the field of,

41

application, scholarship of, 76

Asian Americans faculty

promotion rates are higher than the overall promotion rates

for all faculty, 22

employment of, 17

Astin (1984) psychosocial models of faculty productivity, 48

Astin and Milem (1997), academic men with an academic spouse

less productive than those with a nonacademic spouse, 67

audience for monograph, 1

Average Faculty Publication Rates, 7–8

classics in the field of anthropology
 only one was authored by a woman, 41
cognitive or scientific authority, 54
Cole and Singer (1991),
 model of limited differences, 64
 productivity puzzle of, 71
collaboration through co-authorship
 as one important source of reinforcement, 55
collegial networks
 importance of, 56
 need for research on extent that sex and race segregated,
  81
Collins (1986) "informed outsider," 51
Committee on the Status of Women in the Economics Profession,
 38
Communications, criteria for assessing publishing productivity in, 6
Conceptual Explanations associated with publishing productivity
 for gender differences in the environmental factors, 54
 for gender related correlates, 47
converging publishing rates among men and women, 15
Criteria that systematically block the Promotion of women and
 minorities, 74–75
criteria used to measure publishing productivity, 5
Critical Events Associated with Prolific Publishing
  that vary by gender, 64
Critique of Citations, 41–42
culturally defined stereotypes about gender implicit in definition
 of science as impersonal, objective and universal, 73
Cumulative Advantage and productivity
 in Environmental Factors associated with Publishing , 57–58
 as *how* faculty are able to initiate and sustain research, 57
current academic compensation tend to recognize male strengths
 and female weaknesses, 73
Current Contents, 41

D
"decay curve," 65
Deconstructing the language of Faculty Productivity, 71–73
Developing Distinct Performance Standards by Academic Field, 78
differences in gender may not appear over short periods of time,
 14
disciplines with highest average career publication rates, 10
discovery, scholarship of, 76

distinguished faculty by virtue of their publication records
are those who have a work assignment suited to it, 82
Dwyer, Flynn, and Inman (1991) comprehensive review presents
conceptual explanations for gender differences, 47

E
Economics
criteria used to assess publishing productivity, 6
ten most cited authors in, 37
Elmore and Blackburn (1983) found no significant differences in
three-year publication rates of black and white faculty, 18
English, gender gap in publication productivity narrowed between
1969 and 1988 in, 8
environmental factors
point to the characteristics external to the institution, 47–48
ERIC Clearinghouse, criteria of being referenced through, 77
essential for women to be taken seriously
external validation through recognition by senior rank, 68

F
factors associated with head start on a faculty career
more readily identifiable than those that sustain it, 70
Faculty Publication Rates
affected by acceptance rates of journals in academic field, 11
increase, 9
faculty publishing productivity
major implications for strategies to evaluate, 44–45
subject of book, 2
Finkelstein (1984) current academic compensation
tend to recognize male strengths and female weaknesses,
73
Fox (1985) analysis of correlates of faculty production without
exploration how vary by gender, 47
Fox (1995) summarize individual and environmental factors
associated with aspects of career attainment, 47

G
Garland (1990) use of normalized weighted score, 32
Gender and
Citation Rates, 38–41
Measures of Publishing Productivity, 38
probably race or ethnicity, influence publishing productivity
indirectly through four key variables, 47

prolific publishing, 16
Publishing Productivity, 13–16
Gender differences
    explanations regarding impact of publishing productivity
      and rewards, 25–28
    among the prolific, 65–66
      biggest difference is in timing of critical events, 66
    in Mean Journal article productivity, 7
    in productivity explained by series of small disadvantages,
      58
    in the Institutional Factors Associated with Publishing
      Productivity, 51
    major conceptual explanations for factors associated with
      Publishing Productivity, 49
gender
    is a significant predictor of salary, 24
    not a predictor or cause of publishing performance, 15
Graham and Diamond (1997) measures used to determine institutional rankings, 72
Grant, Linda, 2

H
"hard" sciences, 10
Health science faculty have highest average number of career
  refereed journals articles, 10
HERI. *See* Higher Education Research Institute
higher education
    most cited authors in journals of, 36–37
    ten most cited authors in, 37
Higher Education Research Institute, 7
    Faculty Survey, 9
Highly Cited Authors, 36–38
Hispanic promotion rates
    lower than the overall promotion rates for all faculty, 22
Hispanic faculty employment, 17
How faculty Sustain Publishing Productivity, 66–69
    Cumulative advantage, 69
    Environmental factors-recognition, 68–69
    Environmental factors-reinforcement, 69
    individual and environmental characteristic-authority, 67–68
    individual characteristic-lifestyle, 66–67
    Institutional reward structures, 67
    resources, 68

I

Individual Characteristics
    associated with publishing productivity, 48–50
individual factors highlight characteristics of the individual
    producer as being central, 47
inequality in science equitable or inequitable?, 82
"informed outsider," women as being the, 51
initial faculty appointment
    as a second factor instrumental in subsequent rewards, 23
Institute for Scientific Information, 31
institutional factors
    point to characteristics of the department and institution, 47
    Resources, 51–53
    Reward, 50–51
institutional location
    and publishing productivity, strong relationship between, 52
    has the strongest impact where research requires substantial
        material resources, 15
institutional rankings
    Graham and Diamond (1997) measures used to determine,
        72
Institutional Rewards, 22
integration, scholarship of, 76
ISI. See Institute for Scientific Information

J

journal articles
    count rather than books in most academic areas, 72
Journalism
    gender differences in Mean Journal Article Productivity, 7
Journalism & mass communication educators publishing
    productivity
    criteria used to assess in, 6
    significant gender differences among, 14
journal space shortage depresses faculty publishing levels in some
    academic fields, 9

K

Keller (1991) culturally defined stereotypes about gender implicit in
    science as impersonal, objective and universal, 73
key variables
    in influence publishing productivity indirectly, 47
Kirsch (1993)

having authority entails being perceived as an authority, 50
use of, 2
Writing the Academy, 66

L

length of time it takes for idea to be disseminated
    calculated by the number of years until citations peak, 33–34
library and information sciences faculty has no
    significant gender differences in publishing productivity, 14
library faculty with significant gender differences in publishing
    productivity report among, 14
Library Sciences
    criteria used to assess publishing productivity in, 6
    gender differences in Mean Journal Article Productivity, 7
Liebowitz and Palmer (1988)
    ten most cited authors in Economics, 37–38
"limited differences"
    theory, 57
    model, 64
Long, J. Scott, 2
Long (1990) gender differences in productivity
    explained by series of small disadvantages, 58
Long and Fox (1995) "To what extent is the inequality in science
    equitable or inequitable?", 82
low-consensus fields need broader investigation of faculty
    performance in, 79
Lutz (1990) determined that female anthropologists produced about
    one-fourth of the publications, 38–39

M

Marriage and Children as explanation of differences
    in women's productivity and institutional rewards, 26–28
Marriage and Publishing Productivity
    summary of research about relationship between, 27
"Matthew Effect," 68
measuring quantity of publications, 31–33
men's publications versus women's publications
    more female citations classics were books, 41
Merton norms of science, 4
    does evidence from research literature support one of the
        four norms of science proposed by, 21
minority faculty characteristics
    associated with low levels of publishing productivity, 17

N

National Center for Research
    to Improve Post-secondary Teaching and Learning, 7
National Faculty Directory, 36
National Survey of Faculty, 9, 22
NCRIPTAL. *See* National Center for Research to Improve Post-
    secondary Teaching and Learning
negative impart of delay on promotion for women, 23
negative "kicks," 57
Nettles and Perna (1995) found no significant differences in career
    publishing productivity of white, African American, and Asian
    American/Pacific Islander faculty, 18
Non publishers, 8–9

O

organization of book, 2–3
"the outer circle," women as being in, 51

P

Park (1996) traditional criteria for faculty productivity
    function to distinguish between men and women, 4
Pearson (1985) findings, 18.
Percentage of faculty Women and Men by Level of Journal Article
    Productivity and by Institutional Type, 12
performance criteria
  that value the credential of a diverse faculty, 78–79
Physical Education
    criteria used to assess publishing productivity in, 6
    gender differences in Mean Journal Article Productivity, 7
    no significant gender differences in publishing productivity,
      14
prestige of journals, 41
prestige of the doctoral program not a significant predictor of
  career publishing productivity, 58
productivity
    factors that effect, xi–xii
    product of the interaction of individual qualities and
      environmental conditions, 49
"productivity puzzle," 8
    of Cole and Singer (1991), 71
Productivity Rates of Prolific Faculty, 12–13
"professional vulnerability" of women, 49–50

prolific authors as those who have produced enough journal articles to be in the top three to five percent of all faculty in their field, 63

prolific faculty
    account for majority of publications in an academic field, 13

prolific scholars, 12

prolific writer, sustained dedication to scholarly publishing of, 65

promotion rates for minorities, 22

psychology gender gap in publication productivity
    narrowed between 1969 and 1988 in, 8

publication output, 7
    source of data used to calculate, 5

Publication Rates by Field, 9–12

Publishing Productivity, 5-7
    and Rate of Promotion, 22–23
    and salary, 23–24
    criteria used to assess, 6
    need studies of how operate over a career, 80
    not exclusively the product of individual qualities, 3–4
    scholarly productivity when what is actually meant is, 72

"publish or perish mentality," cynicism about the, 71

purpose of monograph, 1–2

Q

quality and quantity and institutional rewards, 24–25

quality scholarship, lack of agreement on what constitutes, 25

quantity rather than quality of publications
    more likely to influence institutional rewards, 24

R

race and publishing productivity, 16–18

race or ethnicity difference in publishing productivity
    articles on, 17–18

racial differences in publishing productivity disappear when
    comparison is limited to faculty in same discipline at similar
        institutions at similar points of the career, 18

Recognition, 48
    as a category in Environmental Factors associated with
        Publishing Productivity, 53–54
    not an element of the institutional reward structure but of
        the broader, collegial environment, 21
    or Visibility, 21–22

Sonnert and Holton (1995 a & b) summarize individual and
    environmental factors associated with career attainment, 47
source index, 31
"survivors" of initial disadvantage, tenured faculty women as, 58
Sustaining Publishing Productivity. *See* How faculty Sustain
    Publishing Productivity.
symbolic capital, citations as a form of, 34

T
teaching, scholarship of, 76
temporary or adjunct faculty position appointment having long-
    term negative impact on career publishing productivity, 60
tenured faculty women as "survivors" of initial disadvantage, 58
traditional criteria for faculty productivity
        function to distinguish between men and women, 4
Trimbur's Foreword to Writing the Academy, 66

U
unidimensional standard of faculty performance
        question why institutions continue to cling to, 82
Universalism, 81
        two aspects of, 4
unpublished documents, use in productivity measures, 33
Usefulness, 76–77
        as basis for further work by other scientists, 33

W
Wanner et al. (1981), relationship between race and career produc-
    tivity disappeared in social sciences and humanities but statisti-
    cally significant in the natural sciences, 18
Ward, Kathryn B., 2
Ward and Grant (1985) "use of paradigms, concepts, models, and
    methods which distort women's experience," 72
Ward and Grant (1996) comprehensive review of the literature
    presents conceptual explanations for gender differences, 47
weighted counts use to access publication productivity, 32
women
        and minorities concentrated in academic areas where
            journal article publication is not generally very high, 10
        as senior authors, 39–40
        authors greater presence among book than journal articles,
            80
        more likely to be influenced by institutional rewards, 50

ASHE-ERIC HIGHER EDUCATION REPORTS

Since 1983, the Association for the Study of Higher Education (ASHE) and the Educational Resources Information Center (ERIC) Clearinghouse on Higher Education, a sponsored project of the Graduate School of Education and Human Development at The George Washington University, have cosponsored the ASHE-ERIC Higher Education Report series. This volume is the twenty-sixth overall and the ninth to be published by the Graduate School of Education and Human Development at The George Washington University.

Each monograph is the definitive analysis of a tough higher education problem, based on thorough research of pertinent literature and institutional experiences. Topics are identified by a national survey. Noted practitioners and scholars are then commissioned to write the reports, with experts providing critical reviews of each manuscript before publication.

Eight monographs (10 before 1985) in the ASHE-ERIC Higher Education Report series are published each year and are available on individual and subscription bases. To order, use the order form on the last page of this book.

Qualified persons interested in writing a monograph for the ASHE-ERIC Higher Education Report series are invited to submit a proposal to the National Advisory Board. As the preeminent literature review and issue analysis series in higher education, the Higher Education Reports are guaranteed wide dissemination and national exposure for accepted candidates. Execution of a monograph requires at least a minimal familiarity with the ERIC database, including *Resources in Education* and the current *Index to Journals in Education*. The objective of these reports is to bridge conventional wisdom with practical research. Prospective authors are strongly encouraged to call Dr. Fife at (800) 773-3742.

For further information, write to
    ASHE-ERIC Higher Education Report Series
    The George Washington University
    One Dupont Circle, Suite 630
    Washington, DC 20036-1183
Or phone (202) 296-2597 ext. 13;
toll free: (800) 773-ERIC ext. 13.

Write or call for a complete catalog.

Visit our Web site at **www.gwu.edu/~eriche/Reports**

CONSULTING EDITORS

Sandra Beyer
University of Texas at El Paso

Robert Boice
State University of New York–Stony Brook

John M. Braxton
Peabody College, Vanderbilt University

Ivy E. Broder
The American University

Nevin C. Brown
The Education Trust, Inc.

Shirley M. Clark
Oregon State System of Higher Education

Robert A. Cornesky
Cornesky and Associates, Inc.

John W. Creswell
Teachers College, University of Nebraska–Lincoln

Rhonda Martin Epper
State Higher Education Executive Officers

Cheryl Falk
Yakima Valley Community College

Mary Frank Fox
Georgia Institute of Technology

Anne H. Frank
American Association of University Professors

Michelle D. Gilliard
Consortium for the Advancement of Private Higher
  Education–The Council of Independent Colleges

Linda Grant
University of Georgia

Arthur Greenberg
Community School District 25, Flushing, New York

Dean L. Hubbard
Northwest Missouri State University

Edward Johnson
Arizona Commission for Post Seconday Education

Patricia M. King
Bowling Green State University

Lisa R. Lattuca
The Spencer Foundation, Chicago, Illinois

Daniel T. Layzell
MGT of America, Inc., Madison, Wisconsin

J. Scott Long
Indiana University

Clara M. Lovett
Northern Arizona University

Laurence R. Marcus
Rowan College

Robert Menges
Northwestern University

Diane E. Morrison
Centre for Curriculum, Transfer, and Technology

L. Jackson Newell
University of Utah

Steven G. Olswang
University of Washington

Laura W. Perna
Frederick D. Patterson Research
  Institute of the College Fund/UNCF

Anne S. Pruit
Council of Graduate Schools

R. Eugene Rice
American Association for Higher Education

Sherry Sayles-Folks
Eastern Michigan University

Jack H. Schuster
Claremont Graduate School–Center for Educational Studies

Marilla D. Svinicki
University of Texas–Austin

David Sweet
OERI, U.S. Department of Education

Jon E. Travis
Texas A&M University

Dan W. Wheeler
University of Nebraska–Lincoln

Donald H. Wulff
University of Washington

Manta Yorke
Liverpool John Moores University

REVIEW PANEL

Richard Alfred
University of Michigan

Robert J. Barak
Iowa State Board of Regents

Alan Bayer
Virginia Polytechnic Institute and State University

John P. Bean
Indiana University–Bloomington

John M. Braxton
Peabody College, Vanderbilt University

Ellen M. Brier
Tennessee State University

Dennis Brown
University of Kansas

Patricia Carter
University of Michigan

John A. Centra
Syracuse University

Paul B. Chewning
Council for the Advancement and Support of Education

Arthur W. Chickering
Vermont College

Darrel A. Clowes
Virginia Polytechnic Institute and State University

Deborah M. DiCroce
Piedmont Virginia Community College

Dorothy E. Finnegan
The College of William & Mary

Kenneth C. Green
Claremont Graduate University

James C. Hearn
University of Georgia

Edward R. Hines
Illinois State University

Deborah Hunter
University of Vermont

Linda K. Johnsrud
University of Hawaii at Manoa

Bruce Anthony Jones
University of Missouri–Columbia

Elizabeth A. Jones
West Virginia University

Marsha V. Krotseng
State College and University Systems of West Virginia

George D. Kuh
Indiana University–Bloomington

J. Roderick Lauver
Planned Systems International, Inc.–Maryland

Daniel T. Layzell
MGT of America, Inc., Madison, Wisconsin

Patrick G. Love
Kent State University

Meredith Jane Ludwig
Education Statistics Services Institute

Mantha V. Mehallis
Florida Atlantic University

Toby Milton
Essex Community College

John A. Muffo
Virginia Polytechnic Institute and State University

L. Jackson Newell
Deep Springs College

Mark Oromaner
Hudson Community College

James C. Palmer
Illinois State University

Robert A. Rhoads
Michigan State University

G. Jeremiah Ryan
Quincy College

Mary Ann Danowitz Sagaria
The Ohio State University

Kathryn Nemeth Tuttle
University of Kansas

RECENT TITLES

Volume 26 ASHE-ERIC Higher Education Reports

1. Faculty Workload Studies: Perspectives, Needs, and Future Directions
   Katrina A. Meyer

Volume 25 ASHE-ERIC Higher Education Reports

1. A Culture for Academic Excellence: Implementing the Quality Principles in Higher Education
   Jann E. Freed, Marie R. Klugman, and Jonathan D. Fife

2. From Discipline to Development: Rethinking Student Conduct in Higher Education
   Michael Dannells

3. Academic Controversy: Enriching College Instruction through Intellectual Conflict
   David W. Johnson, Roger T. Johnson, and Karl A. Smith

4. Higher Education Leadership: Analyzing the Gender Gap
   Luba Chliwniak

5. The Virtual Campus: Technology and Reform in Higher Education
   Gerald C. Van Dusen

6. Early Intervention Programs: Opening the Door to Higher Education
   Robert H. Fenske, Christine A. Geranios, Jonathan E. Keller, and David E. Moore

7. The Vitality of Senior Faculty Members: Snow on the Roof—Fire in the Furnace
   Carole J. Bland and William H. Bergquist

8. A National Review of Scholastic Achievement in General Education: How Are We Doing and Why Should We Care?
   Steven J. Osterlind

Volume 24 ASHE-ERIC Higher Education Reports

1. Tenure, Promotion, and Reappointment: Legal and Administrative Implications
   Benjamin Baez and John A. Centra

2. Taking Teaching Seriously: Meeting the Challenge of Instructional Improvement
   Michael B. Paulsen and Kenneth A. Feldman

3. Empowering the Faculty: Mentoring Redirected and Renewed
   Gaye Luna and Deborah L. Cullen

4. Enhancing Student Learning: Intellectual, Social, and Emotional Integration
   Anne Goodsell Love and Patrick G. Love

5. Benchmarking in Higher Education: Adapting Best Practices to Improve Quality
   Jeffrey W. Alstete

Volume 22 ASHE-ERIC Higher Education Reports

1. The Department Chair: New Roles, Responsibilities, and Challenges
   Alan T. Seagren, John W. Creswell, and Daniel W. Wheeler

2. Sexual Harassment in Higher Education: From Conflict to Community
   Robert O. Riggs, Patricia H. Murrell, and JoAnne C. Cutting

3. Chicanos in Higher Education: Issues and Dilemmas for the 21st Century
   Adalberto Aguirre, Jr., and Ruben O. Martinez

4. Academic Freedom in American Higher Education: Rights, Responsibilities, and Limitations
   Robert K. Poch

5. Making Sense of the Dollars: The Costs and Uses of Faculty Compensation
   Kathryn M. Moore and Marilyn J. Amey

6. Enhancing Promotion, Tenure, and Beyond: Faculty Socialization as a Cultural Process
   William G. Tierney and Robert A. Rhoads

7. New Perspectives for Student Affairs Professionals: Evolving Realities, Responsibilities, and Roles
   Peter H. Garland and Thomas W. Grace

8. Turning Teaching into Learning: The Role of Student Responsibility in the Collegiate Experience
   Todd M. Davis and Patricia Hillman Murrell

ORDER FORM

Quantity   **Amount**

_____ Please begin my subscription to the current year's
         ASHE-ERIC Higher Education Reports at $120.00, over
         33% off the cover price, starting with Report 1.   _____

_____ Please send a complete set of Volume ___ *ASHE-ERIC*
         Higher Education Reports at $120.00, over 33% off the
         cover price.   _____

Individual reports are available for $24.00 and include the cost of shipping and handling.

SHIPPING POLICY:

• Books are sent UPS Ground or equivalent. For faster delivery, call for charges.
• Alaska, Hawaii, U.S. Territories, and Foreign Countries, please call for shipping information.
• Order will be shipped within 24 hours after receipt of request.
• Orders of 10 or more books, call for shipping information.

All prices shown are subject to change.

Returns: No cash refunds—credit will be applied to future orders.

PLEASE SEND ME THE FOLLOWING REPORTS:

Quantity	Volume/No.	Title	Amount

Please check one of the following: **Subtotal:** _____

☐ Check enclosed, payable to GW-ERIC.

☐ Purchase order attached.   **Less Discount:** _____

☐ Charge my credit card indicated below: **Total Due:** _____

  ☐ Visa   ☐ MasterCard

Expiration Date_____

Name_____

Title_____

Institution _____

Address_____

City _____ State _____ Zip_____

Phone _____ Fax _____Telex_____

Signature _____ Date_____

SEND ALL ORDERS TO: ASHE-ERIC Higher Education Reports
The George Washington University
One Dupont Cir., Ste. 630, Washington, DC 20036-1183
Phone: (202) 296-2597 ext. 13
Toll-free: (800) 773-ERIC ext. 13
FAX: (202) 452-1844
URL: www.gwu.edu/~eriche/Reports